The Book of Bauer

The Book of Bauer

Stories from a Forgotten Town

Stephen S. Lottridge

The University of Utah Press
Salt Lake City

The Defiance House Man colophon is a registered trademark of
the University of Utah Press. It is based on a four-foot-tall Ancient
Puebloan pictograph (late PIII) near Glen Canyon, Utah.

LIBRARY OF CONGRESS CATALOGING-IN-PUBLICATION DATA

Names: Lottridge, Stephen S. (Stephen Stuart), 1936- author.
Title: The book of Bauer : stories from a forgotten town / Stephen S. Lottridge.
Description: Salt Lake City : The University of Utah Press, [2024] | Short
stories. | Summary: "Graffiti-covered industrial concrete ruins are all
that remain today to remind us of the lives, adventures, and human
relationships that once animated Bauer, Utah. Located just south of
Tooele, across the Oquirrh Mountains west of the Salt Lake Valley, Bauer
was abandoned in 1979 and declared a toxic waste site. The Book of
Bauer: Stories from a Forgotten Town brings it back to life, evoking
mid-twentieth century family and community in that company town as seen
through the eyes of an observant adolescent boy. Presenting a dramatic
snapshot of life in Bauer in narrative autobiographical form, the book
recalls the fate of hundreds of derelict mining towns throughout the
mountain and sagebrush West. With vivid prose and intimate observation,
The Book of Bauer offers an unparalleled memoir of small-town life in
Utah and the Great Basin"—Provided by publisher.
Identifiers: LCCN 2023036716 |
ISBN 9781647691455 (paperback) | ISBN 9781647691462 (ebook)
Subjects: LCSH: Lottridge, Stephen S. (Stephen Stuart), 1936—Childhood
and youth. | Teenage boys—Utah—Biography. | Bauer (Utah)—Biography.
Classification: LCC PS3612.O77778 Z46 2023 | DDC 818/.603
[B]—dc23/eng/20231115
LC record available at https://lccn.loc.gov/2023036716

Errata and further information on this and other titles
available at UofUpress.com

Printed and bound in the United States of America.

Contents

Prologue   vii

1 Sailing on the Guppy Pond   1

2 My Sister Had an Arvin Radio   13

3 Not Kissing Carol Druby Good Night   29

4 Mr. Bunn's Horses   37

5 Oatmeal, Not Black-Eyed Peas   51

6 Setting Mr. Perks's Lawn on Fire   65

7 Why I Did Not Become an Eagle Scout but How
I Did Get Invited to the Ninth-Grade Prom   74

8 Seeing If I Could Kill My Father   88

9 Blowing Up Bauer   94

10 Bull Snakes by the Furnace   103

11 Armed Hikes and Baseball   110

12 Sporty   121

Epilogue   133

Acknowledgments   141
About the Author   143

Illustrations follow page 60

Prologue

Bauer, Utah, no longer exists. Oh, rubble remains. Relics of houses, bits of foundation, a scattering of broken boards clutter the area. Foul spreads of old tailings from the lead mine, sulfur seeps, and residue from the resin plant deaden the desert flats. Oxygen cans, fallen from their destroyed bins, serve as rifle targets. Bullet marks pock the graffiti-covered remnants of concrete and stone structures.

Essentially, Bauer has gone the way of all towns that disappear. Lakes behind huge dams drown many. Urban expansion or commercial development absorbs or razes others. As with Bauer, all residents eventually forsake their homes when the sole source of employment dies. When the last person has fled, the boneyard lies exposed to weather and human abuse.

The Environmental Protection Agency (EPA) has declared Bauer a toxic waste site. Arsenic and lead leach into the sparse water and blow in wind from dried-up holding ponds and tailing piles. However, attempts to block public access have proved useless. Vandals tore down the gate and fencing across the access road. Evidence of drug use marks the old Honerine Mine tunnel. Clandestine paintball teams hold battles and tournaments in the overgrown ruins.

Earliest records tell us that soldiers stationed in Stockton, Utah, began mining in what came to be known as Bauer in the 1860s. They dug the Honerine Tunnel to extract lead and silver. Eventually, civilian corporations took over the business and established a milling operation on-site. They founded a company town to accommodate the workers and their families.

Not as large as Stockton or nearby Tooele—some three miles down the road—Bauer still prospered modestly for several decades. Never a real town, but always a settlement with few amenities, Bauer depended entirely on the local mine, mill, and eventually other metallurgical enterprises for its existence. Over time, these companies came to use the surroundings as unregulated dumping grounds for dangerous and untreated industrial waste, and the population dwindled. The last residents abandoned their houses in 1979, when the final plant, owned by the Blackhawk Resin Company, shut down. Fire destroyed the last of the works in 1980, and officials ordered the site closed.

None of this information, accurate as it may be, calls to mind the place my family lived in for a year, from August 1950 to August 1951. It's true, even as recently as that year, no store, gas station, church, school, restaurant, or other amenities graced the settlement. A small boardinghouse, run by the local rancher's wife, provided meals for a few of the underground miners and some of the plant workers and supervisors. The Pioche Mines Company owned Bauer;

it provided us rent-free accommodations in a ramshackle structure while my father trained in Salt Lake City, some forty-five miles east, for a job he would take up in southern Nevada.

A bus carried my brother, sister, and me the three or so miles to school in Tooele, the closest town, and we shopped there for food and any other supplies as well. Bauer was now barely hanging on. The mine had so fouled the tap water that we could not drink it. We used it to wash our hands, carefully, and to shower without opening our mouths, but a weekly flatbed truck delivered our drinking and cooking water in metal, fifty-gallon containers. We ladled it out, careful not to spill a drop. We never turned on the crusted kitchen tap.

Still, all towns that disappear own a history, not just of dates, data, and decline, but of lives lived. The stories in this collection provide a snapshot of life in a settlement, now derelict and uninhabitable, that once rang with all the struggles and joys of human existence. From the distance of seven-plus decades, Bauer comes alive again in these tales of one year, one family, and one fourteen-year-old boy vital with burgeoning energy, innocent adventure, romance, friendship, and family relations. No place dies completely as long as it exists in vivid memory.

The appropriately misshapen, somewhat triangular guppy pond, where the author and his brother raised the sunken boat and sailed it, lies to the immediate right of center in this photograph. The Honerine Mine building stands just below the pond. The plant and mill works spread beyond it, with the desert flats, where the author and his siblings rode Mr. Bunn's horses, extending to the horizon. The lone road in front of the residential area starts to the right of the far tip of the pond. Stands of cottonwood trees, visible in this picture, surround the houses and provide some comfort and shelter in an otherwise barren landscape. The railroad line running from Tooele to Stockton crosses in the foreground. While this image was taken some twenty-seven years before the author moved to Bauer, the settlement looks much the same as it did when these stories are set.

1

Sailing on the Guppy Pond

A hot burst of wind surged against the sail, and the unwieldy skiff lurched away from the bank, stem down. My brother, Doug, and I perched on the stern plate, the narrow edge cutting into my buttocks, our feet braced against the after thwart. We hiked back as far as we could without falling overboard, using our weight to keep the prow from nosing under. Without a rudder, the stern yawed in the swirling wind. We awkwardly guided our craft, dragging poles port and starboard, shifting our bodies as the boat heeled. The bow plowed through the weed-choked water until it curved into the narrow slip by the sluice gate on the far shore, at the pond's outlet some one hundred fifty feet from our starting point. Exhilarated by our success, we clambered out, painter in hand, and prepared for another cruise.

Doug and I had resurrected that hulk soon after we arrived in Bauer. We had been exploring the unpromising environs of our house, one of fifteen spread along two dirt tracks uphill from the mine and plant that comprised the sole source of work in the arid area. The skiff was a twelve-foot, lapstrake, two-thwart, blunt-bowed, decrepit wooden rowboat, missing tholes, oarlocks and, needless to say, oars themselves. We had first spotted it submerged in the murky shallows, waterlogged and algae-coated—a derelict.

My fourteenth birthday came around in October of 1950, and Doug turned thirteen the following August. No other boys our age lived in Bauer, so the situation threw us on our own resources for activities and entertainment. Our first glimpse of the pond discouraged us. We had just left the Bitterroot Mountains in the far northern Idaho panhandle, where we had imprinted on evergreen forests, clear-running streams and blue lakes of trout. Had we found such an alternative here, we would have passed up this open-air sump with one look. But we were resourceful, and life offered adventure whatever the circumstances.

The lakelet, fed by the mouth of the mine, reeked of sulfur. Profuse weeds clogged the water, swaying languidly as the tepid flow tugged at them. Scum covered much of the surface, moving from one end of the pond to the other as the wind shifted direction. Thousands of guppies wriggled and swarmed through the submerged vegetation, evidently without predators. Near the outlet sluice gate, now lacking much of the wood that had originally impeded the current, we stood, assessing. Then we spied the outlines of the boat through the brown liquid, and began to plan.

We led my father down to have a look. Through him, the plant manager gave us hesitant, conditional permission to resurrect the craft. I imagine he thought the enterprise quixotic, but was willing to do my father the favor. More importantly, he stated his terms: no impeding traffic on the road below the outlet; no other people to participate at any time; no wandering farther onto the plant grounds or into the mine; no using company materials; and the company had complete absolution from any and all responsibility or liability if we were to be injured on company property. These terms we readily agreed to, from a combination of innocence and enthusiasm. I could not imagine any damage we could do beyond what nature, neglect and man-made pollution had already wrought.

Raising the boat, such as it was, demanded thought and effort. Its size and position prevented us from simply climbing in and dragging it out. Equipping ourselves with a shovel, rake and some hemp rope, we set about the task. Standing on the bank, we managed to cut and clear some of the weeds and willow roots ensnaring the bow and scrape some of the accumulated slime from the small foredeck, the gunwales and forward thwart. With the shovel, we cleared a small slip beside the sluice gate where we could slide the craft in and out.

Repellent though the water appeared, it became obvious that one of us would have to wade in to attach the rope. We hemmed and hawed and negotiated until, as the elder and stronger, I agreed to enter the fetid liquid. I checked my legs for cuts to avoid absorbing whatever infections or toxins would wash around me.

I briefly thought of my mother's hesitation when we had announced our idea to her. Familiar with the outdoors as she was, she understood and accepted that we would suffer the range of injuries and damage normal for active boys. She did not hover and worry; she calmly bandaged when necessary and occasionally offered advice. Even she, however, after walking down to inspect the pond, turned cautionary. She did not forbid us, but she warned us to be careful and to check in with her often. In contrast, my father expressed no concern whatsoever, only occasional supportive interest.

Taking off my shoes and socks and rolling my trouser legs high up on my thighs, I stepped and slid in, one end of the rope in hand. Ooze squeezed between my toes, and weeds caught at my legs as I felt my way. The smell of rank mud rose around me. Guppies nipped softly at my calves. With one hand I groped around the sodden wood until I found a hole, ran the line through, tied a bowline by feel and backed out. My brother secured the other end of the line around his waist, and we began to tug.

The boat did not budge. Its saturated weight had settled solidly into the mud and vegetation that had grown up around it. While we rested for a moment, I wondered why it had been launched to begin with. Had the pond once been bigger and the water fresh enough to invite a person to fish? The hull had clearly lain there for years. We tried again, this time putting our backs fully into it, with the same result.

As we let the line go slack, a counterintuitive idea popped into my mind. What if, instead of pulling, we pushed and dislodged the boat that way? Once we freed it from its bonds, we might then be able to heave it onto dry land.

(Only later, as a psychologist, did I learn about Erick Erickson's paradoxical interventions.) Jabbing the shovel blade into the soft wood, I leaned on the handle and pushed. After a moment, I felt the boat give slightly and move a few inches deeper along the bottom.

Excited, we hauled on the line again and the hulk came toward us, a little beyond where it had formerly lain, before briefly getting stuck again. Back and forth we went, pushing and pulling, until finally the bow began to break the surface and the whole boat rose, water pouring over the stern plate and gunwales as the nose came up the slip onto the bank and road. We rocked the hull, splashing liquid, weeds and guppies onto the dirt until the boat was light enough for us to turn over and drain. Rolling it back onto its keel, we dragged it to the other side of the outlet, inverted it again and laid it on a patch of gravelly ground beside the road to dry out. We did not spot any obvious holes in the hull or cracks in the strakes, but I knew enough about watercraft to understand that we needed to let it dry before we could tell if it needed caulking or other repairs.

As we had been working, a few trucks and pedestrians had passed. The drivers would answer our waves but did not stop. One passerby asked disapprovingly if we knew we were on company property, and grunted doubtfully when we said we had permission. But a couple of others took a benign interest. None of them had realized a sunken boat lay there; they commended our efforts and wished us well. One said, as he headed for the plant gate, that it might liven up the place.

We checked on the boat frequently. We did not think of it as ours, exactly, since it belonged to the Pioche Mines Company, sort of, but we thought of it as ours to use on loan since we had resurrected it. We took a proprietary and protective interest in it without becoming attached. We might have felt differently if the craft had been more prepossessing; as it was, the relationship remained transactional.

School demands and other activities intervened, but one late-September Saturday, when we thought the wood had dried, we decided to give the boat a shakedown cruise and do any necessary caulking and carpentry before bad weather set in. It looked trimmer after we had cleaned it, and a small cubby in the bow suggested that it had once been a homey little craft. Still, I fully expected water to come leaking through the hull when we set it afloat, and imagined it swamped again.

I knotted the painter on, we slid the boat stern first down the slip and let it drift out from the bank. It bobbed slightly and swung around when the wind ruffled the water. I watched carefully for some time, but the waterline rose no higher. I tugged it to shore, but saw no water inside the hull.

Buoyed, we decided to risk climbing aboard. I fetched a pole from the garage and we pushed off. Accustomed to canoes, we quickly sat on the thwarts along the centerline. Even with our weight, the wind drove the boat when it caught the freeboard, and my attempts to direct it with the pole proved awkward and ineffective. The end of the pole stuck in the mucky bottom, and the boat listed when

I lifted it free. Later in life, I read about the English art of punting, but this scow responded to no such skill, and my novice wielding would not have directed even a sleek punt accurately on a still day.

By now, the breeze had lodged us in a willow thicket. Gingerly trading places with my brother, I knelt on the deck of the cubby, backed us out onto open water and laboriously, alternating sides, half-paddled, half-pulled us back to the slip. Once on land, we beached the boat, keel up, well away from the road, under some bushes, and left it, unsure of our next move.

For the rest of the fall and over the winter, other occupations commanded our attention. We hunted and hiked. Sometimes we drove into Salt Lake City. I studied hard and spent hours with my electric train. In the winter, we skied on the hill behind the house. Still, the boat stayed in my memory. I walked down to check on it from time to time, sometimes finding it buried under an oblong of snow.

Come summer vacation, we checked to see how the boat had weathered our version of dry dock. It seemed no worse for its spell in the roadside bushes, but the problem that had nagged me on and off during the winter came into focus when we turned it over. How to navigate it? I had mentally diagrammed a way either to attach tholes to the gunwales or to restore the splintered holes for oarlocks. The wood was too damaged for the former, and, in any case, we had no oars, with or without locks.

A rush of wind ruffled the water and with it came the thought: let's rig a sailboat. The memory of clumsily poling and pulling made the idea of letting the wind do at least some of the work immediately appeal to me. I had dreamed of sailing; now might be the opportunity. My initial enthusiasm faded as I examined the inside of the hull and the forward thwart and surveyed the water. Although the craft had not leaked the previous fall, the strakes and deck boards had splintered during the winter, and I doubted we could fix a mast successfully. The pond was small and the craft unwieldy; I questioned whether we could come about and tack into the wind. Also, I did not want to put much energy or time into repairs or improvements, since we would be leaving at the end of the summer.

We jerry-rigged a compromise. We dug out a pair of two-by-fours from the pile of lumber in the loft of the old garage. We sawed them to equal lengths, started twenty-penny nails at equal intervals along both and nailed them fast to the after side of the forward thwart and to the insides of the port and starboard gunwales. Given the curve of the hull, these "masts" rose at an angle, wider apart at the top than at the bottom. We begged a worn flannel bedsheet from our mother, pierced holes in the long edges to correspond to the separation of the small nails and wound makeshift grommets with masking and electrical tape. We were set.

I should mention that a flock of hostile domestic geese attended—and impeded—our work. They often congregated in front of the gate to the plant, blocking the footpath and hissing aggressively. We asked around, but no one claimed ownership, including Mr. and Mrs. Bunn, the local rancher and his wife. At first, I thought the geese might be upset because we were disturbing their nest on the pond, but they didn't attack when we were on the water. We never saw them swim there. They had the run of the settlement but seemed to prefer the area around the pond and boarding-house. They treated everyone with ill will but responded to our presence with particular pugnacity.

The gander treated us more tolerantly, and sometimes wandered off when the goose came at us with singular ferocity. They had a large brood of goslings that year, several of whom, after they had fledged, joined their mother in lunging and whipping their beaks at us. After the first few encounters, I took to carrying a stick with me to ward off these anserine assaults. But the weapon seemed to enrage the goose even more. Her upstretched neck made her almost as tall as I was, and the black lance of her bill as she struck toward me flared as dangerous as a dirk.

She did not manage to wound either my brother or me, but she guarded the gate with combative zeal. She and her brood troubled Doug less than they did me; fear held me more tightly, in general. More than once, she followed me as I backed away, stick held horizontally in front of me. I suspected that she sensed my fright.

I dreamed of whacking her, breaking her neck or bash-ing in her skull. When I mentioned my vision to my father, he cautioned me not to counterattack.

"They must belong to someone," he said. "We don't want to have to deal with an irate owner of barnyard fowl."

I heeded his admonition and did not go on the offensive, much as I longed to. I confined the idea to my daydreams,

9

which came to include roast goose for dinner and a pillow of goose down.

Doug and I became a common sight on the pond that summer. We left the grommets attached to the nails on the starboard "mast" when we beached the boat for the night. In the days, we poled and paddled our way up from the slip to the willows at the far end of the pond and turned our craft around. Doug would clutch the willow branches to hold us steady while I fixed the other side of our flannel sail to the port mast. I would retreat to the stern, Doug would let go of the willows, the wind would catch, the bedsheet would grow taut, and off we would launch.

On our first runs, we worked our poles off one beam or the other, aiming for the slip where we could more easily turn the boat. The drag slowed us up, however, and the strain on the sail as we braked threatened to tear the grommets. With experience, we grew more daring and let the wind take us on faster and more exciting, if briefer, rides. Often, we plowed into another bank of willows, where I unhooked the sail as we arduously extricated ourselves, turned and headed back for another unpredictable voyage.

As we became more accustomed to the pond and made it part of our lives, we tried swimming in it. The experience offered minimal pleasure, but it provided a relatively cool respite on a hot summer day. Weeds clung to our limbs, guppies nipped and nibbled, the smell of sulfur and mud swirled around us. We swam with our heads above water, loath to risk dunking in the miasmic fluid. We emerged courageous and triumphant. Once or twice we almost, but not quite, enticed someone else to join us.

August came, and my family left Bauer as planned. Doug and I unrigged the sail and left our craft nosed up in the slip, the painter tied to a bankside bush. By now, I had developed an affection for the clumsy little rowboat. The geese had gone somewhere else when I bade it a peaceful, rueful farewell, wondering if anyone else would prize it and treat it gently.

After I lived for decades on the coasts as a student, adult, professional, and family man, the twists of fate brought me back to the Mountain West. Once there, something drew me to the place of my fourteenth year. I drove to Salt Lake City, to Tooele and out to Bauer. I walked through our old house, its door swinging atilt on broken hinges. Holes gaped in the floor, old plaster and wallpaper draped from the walls, mice scurried, and a bull snake nested by the dead furnace down the broken cellar stairs. Large metal buildings, their gleaming silver stacks belching gray smoke, loomed in the arid distance beyond where the plant had lain. The pond had evaporated to a basin of foul sludge. No sign of our boat remained.

I have sailed many times since that year, on salt water and fresh. I have tacked upwind with ease, the boat heeling as the canvas billowed. Spinnakers have pulled me so fast the whole crew hung over the after rail, the boat dancing to the touch of the rudder. I have paddled responsive canoes that turned with the flick of my wrist. I have rowed sleek dories. Still, behind all those pleasures, dreams of Bauer return—the tug of the wind against the flannel sail, the smell of sulfur, the early adolescent bliss of sailing on the guppy pond.

2

My Sister Had an Arvin Radio

My sister had an Arvin radio. Small and silver, with rounded corners, it looked a little like a miniature tank—without the guns, of course. She had bought the radio herself, with her own money. This must have been in the mid-1940s, several years before we moved to Bauer. How she accumulated the cash I am not sure. I know she babysat sometimes, starting after she turned twelve, and she may have saved some money relatives sent for her birthday or at Christmas. She didn't show the same streaks of frugality and entrepreneurial enterprise that I did, but when she set her mind to something, she did not swerve.

She carried the radio home in a large bag and immediately secreted it and herself in her room. She did not invite any of us in to listen with her. For the next few years, whenever she was home, the sounds of popular music would waft quietly from behind her closed door in the evening.

Shortly before she acquired that Arvin, my brother, sister and I had stayed overnight one Saturday with some friends of my parents. My father belonged to the local Toastmasters club. He and my mother had driven to a regional competition and did not plan to return until well after midnight. While my brother and I tried vainly to amuse ourselves with some old board games that lacked crucial pieces, my sister holed up with the high school-aged daughter of the house to listen to the Saturday night hit parade on the girl's radio. Eventually, the strains of Hoagy Carmichael's "Ole Buttermilk Sky" rang out, climaxing the program, much to my sister's pleasure (we could hear her excited treble). She had told me on the drive over that she hoped the song would continue its extended run at the top of the charts. That evening, huddling together with an older girl, thrilling to the songs, and chatting about popular music persuaded my sister to save up for her own radio.

Having a radio was a big thing back then. Not every household could afford one. Commercial television had not yet become widely available and listening to the radio provided our main connection to the outside world in the small, remote places where we lived. Most every town published its own newspaper, but the radio created a more immediate sense of participating in current events with the rest of the country.

A few years before my sister's Arvin made its nest in her room, my father had appeared one evening with what he triumphantly announced was a present for the family. Taken out of its wrapping, it resembled a large, reddish-brown, rectangular box, with a silvery mesh screen across the middle of one side and prominent, dark brown dials arranged along the bottom. On the back, screws held a perforated tin covering in place. Removing that panel allowed you access to the workings, and the ability to replace tubes when they died.

We lived in the far northern panhandle of Idaho then, in the towns of Mullan and Wallace. Reception came in spottily up there in the mountains. You had to string a long wire antenna up a wall or around the room and sometimes out the window and up onto the roof to catch the signal. My first memory of listening to the family radio dates from the Billy Conn–Joe Louis fight of June 1941. My father and some men from the Morning Mine, where he worked as assistant superintendent, had been adding on a couple of rooms to what had been a tiny house, to accommodate the five of us in our family. The house belonged to the mining company, which was supplying the material, since the addition would increase the value of the property. The men were volunteering their labor; most of the work took place in the lengthening evenings and on weekends. In a gesture of appreciation for their help, my father had invited the workers to stay after they finished that evening, have some coffee and listen to the fight on the new radio.

Perhaps because they were still in their rough clothes and boots, my father, rather than inviting them into the small combination living room-bedroom, which contained only two chairs anyway, brought the radio into the construction area. The framing still opened to the outside air, but a few electrical outlets protruded from the bare inside studs. My father plugged the radio into one of them and placed the set first on the fresh planking and then, at someone's suggestion, on an old crate in the middle of the room. The men sat around on sawhorses and toolboxes, coffee cups in their calloused hands, chatting in anticipation.

After the tubes had warmed up and my father had found the right frequency, everyone leaned forward as the voice of the announcer joined us. But even here, in a space still uncontained by walls or insulation, the distant voice wove in and out. My father fiddled with the dials and picked up the set, turning it this way and that in an effort to improve reception. One or another of the men got up now and then to adjust the antenna when the transmission raveled. Several of them offered confident—and often contradictory—advice on how to adjust the knobs. At a critical juncture, one of them leapt to his feet and climbed up a ladder on the outside of the framing to wind the antenna wire around a nail jutting from a beam.

The announcer's excited tones would slide in, grow loud and intelligible for a while, then fade and cede to the constant static. Most of the men responded animatedly when the voice grew clear, remarking on the progress of the match, then strained quietly to make out the words behind the interference. One man sat quietly the whole time, leaning back against one of the studs, apart, holding his cup in his thin, still hands. I felt uneasy when I looked at him; I wondered if he objected to boxing. I felt ambivalent about it myself, but the energized involvement of the others caught me up in the excitement. In addition, young as I was—I must have been five at the time—my father was including me in this group of men, which excited me as much as the fight itself. Neither my brother nor sister, nor my mother for that matter, shared that privilege.

While I had not heard of either Joe Louis or Billy Conn until a few days before their contest, and I knew little about the world of professional prizefighting, the experience of listening to the broadcast in that company of adult males led me to develop visions of being a boxer. Two years later, at my request, my parents presented me with a pair of boxing gloves for my birthday. The following winter, I prevailed upon my father to take me to tryouts for a newly forming boys boxing club some schoolmates had told me about. I proudly took my own gloves with me, but the organizer insisted on fitting me out with a much larger, softer pair. When my turn came, I could hardly see my opponent behind the giant red cushions attached to my hands. Both of us stood there.

"C'mon, mix it up," the club organizer shouted. I tried a jab, a move I had learned about in conversations with my father and had watched him demonstrate. The soft padding on my hand connected with the matching pillows my sparring partner had raised protectively in front of his face.

"C'mon," came the command again. "The clock's running." Although I had practiced an orderly set of sequential moves at home, no hope remained of deploying them here. Excited and unsteady, I flailed with my feet as I punched blindly away.

The referee immediately seized me from behind and stopped the fight, such as it was, roughly stripped the gloves from my hands, grabbed my arm and plunked me down next to my father, accusing me of trying to kick my opponent. Baffled and ashamed, I denied it, but the referee categorically rejected my appeal. My father did not comment. I understood instinctively that, while he may have agreed with me, he did not want to undermine the referee's authority in front of the other boys.

Thus ended my sole early foray into the sporting world of boxing. (I later sparred a few times with a friend as he was training for a match, but he was practicing blocking punches and did not try to hit me.) I have kept the gloves my parents gave me, stashed in a cardboard box where my mother saved some of my childhood memorabilia.

Out of character as it may otherwise seem to those who know me now, I continued to take a spectator's interest in boxing for many years. People spoke of it as "the manly art of self defense." Sports writers referred to it as the "sweet science." During my two years of junior high in Wallace, my father and I occasionally attended smokers, as local boxing matches were called. I imagined how I would handle my opponent in the bouts I watched, and I even toyed briefly with the prospect of eventually trying out for the high school boxing team.

I did not like fighting in general. The violence, anger and bloody injuries frightened me. I avoided, almost to the point of cowardice, getting involved in schoolyard or playground fistfights, although I sometimes watched them in timid fascination. Once, when I was at a smoker with my father, someone in the doorway shouted, "Fight!" and a third of the spectators raced outside, abandoning the boxing match to watch a street fight. I half stood in my seat, asking my father if we should go, too, drawn morbidly to the image, but he simply nodded at the ring in front of us and pointed to my seat.

Despite my fear of street fighting, though, the idea of organized, regulated combat with gloves appealed to me. I don't know whether or not I would have tried out for the boxing team; we moved to Bauer after my eighth-grade year, and the schools I attended from then on did not offer the sport. The idea, more than the practice, appealed to me, and anyway, the matches took place in winter, when I was already playing basketball, a sport I enjoyed.

For someone with a fairly gentle and sensitive nature, I was drawn toward violent sports in general: boxing, football, rugby. I dreamed of taking up challenging and dangerous work in the future. The idea of being a smoke jumper intrigued me, as I read about the exploits of Hank Winston and Jim Dade in *Boys' Life* magazine. I also idealized marines—the toughest of the tough in my image of warriors. I liked to hunt and shoot guns, and often imagined myself in wartime combat. In all of this, I may have been trying to impress my father, who presented himself as a rugged, fearless man. Or perhaps, and more importantly, those visions and interests expressed the angry, violent part of my being that I otherwise repressed.

As I listened through the static to the excited bursts of narration from the announcer of the Louis–Conn bout, I tried to imagine the arena and the ring and the boxers themselves. In conversations with my father, I had learned that Joe Louis, a Black fighter, held the heavyweight title, which he was defending against the white, light-heavyweight champion, Billy Conn. I had taken a liking to Joe Louis and quietly hoped he would win. Most of the men huddled around the radio that evening, though, were rooting for Billy Conn. At first, their talk was simply evaluative. Not only did Louis weigh more, he stood taller and had a longer reach. They were supporting the underdog.

As the static and the evening wore on, however, and the interpolations of the announcer made it clear that Conn led on points, the tenor of the men's remarks became more partisan, with an edge I did not understand. Their reactions and comments suggested that the stakes in this match involved something larger, more general. Nobody said anything overtly, but the electrified atmosphere developed an undertone that confused and disturbed me. When the last intelligible spate of words from the announcer revealed that Louis had knocked Conn out late in the fight, somewhere in the thirteenth round, as I recall, some of the group members' comments betrayed not just disappointment but also a tinge of bitterness. When they told me the outcome—I could not understand the announcer's words—I cheered. I quickly quieted, however, when none of the men joined in, and some of them looked seriously and questioningly at me and then at my father. The one who had been leaning against the stud, away from the others, smiled briefly as he met my eyes, but kept silent.

My Sister Had an Arvin Radio

Later, in response to my baffled questions, my father clarified why he and the others had not wanted Louis to win. He spoke calmly, without resentment or anger, as he explained that the men had longed to have a white heavyweight champion again. Historically, white men had held the heavyweight title. In the first two decades of the century, Jack Johnson had provided an exception, and many a "white hope" had climbed into the ring unsuccessfully against him. I appreciated my father's explanation, but did not like it. I inquired why color made a difference. He responded by reiterating his original explanation, agreeing that it shouldn't but affirming that it did. I accepted what he told me as true, but I did not understand.

Black athletes were just beginning to come into their own and gain wider recognition at that time. Later in the decade, Jackie Robinson broke the color barrier in major league baseball, and others followed him. As I grew older, I tracked the careers of Louis, Robinson, and other Black athletes. I took an equal interest in the history of Jim Thorpe, the Native American ball player, runner, and Olympic champion. Perhaps because I myself felt like an outsider, despite my obvious privilege as a white male of Anglo-Saxon extraction, the stories of present and historical figures on the fringes of mainstream society attracted and moved me.

My sister acquired her Arvin radio during this period of my development. She evinced no interest in boxing matches, or in any other sporting events. She rarely joined the rest of us when we tuned in to noonday quiz or giveaway programs on the weekends. Ensconced in her room with her own Arvin, she listened to popular music on her favorite AM stations. She tried to engage me in discussions about Perry Como and Frank Sinatra, but my interests lay in sports, books and the natural world, so I proved an unsatisfying conversationalist to her. All the same, I liked hearing the music coming from her room. I never had the luxury of a room to myself; my parents always placed my brother and me together. I envied her privacy; the tunes she played soothed me. When she went away to boarding school for her ninth-grade year, I missed both her and that comfort.

The reddish-brown family box lasted a few years. Smaller, sleeker sets succeeded it. My mother would tune in to accompany her housework. My brother and I would join her during lunch and listen to a program called *Queen for a Day*, which gave away appliances and furniture to the winning contestant. We eagerly, though unsuccessfully, sent in applications for our mother.

Later, in Wallace, I would sit in the dinette just off the kitchen and tune in to the Mutual Broadcasting System's *Game of the Day* with their baseball announcer, Al Helfer. My mother had grown up in Brooklyn as an avid Dodgers fan. She fondly reminisced about her brothers taking her to Ebbets Field to watch the games when she was a young girl. I inherited her enthusiasm for the Dodgers and followed the radio broadcasts of their games when I could, although I often wavered between that passive interest and playing outside in the summer weather. I would become engrossed in evening programs, as well—boys' adventure series such as *Tom Mix*, *Bobby Benson and the B-Bar-B Riders*, and *Sergeant Preston of the Yukon*. Often my mother would be working in the kitchen nearby. Sometimes she would take a break and sit with me. We would comment on the programs or the course of the game, sharing a rare intimate moment alone together.

The first car my parents owned, a 1936 Chevrolet sedan, lacked a radio. On road trips we whiled away the time singing songs and telling stories. I enjoyed that companionship and learned to chime in on the popular tunes from the 1920s that my parents loved. As my sister and brother and I grew into teenagers and became more engaged with popular culture, though, the radio assumed greater importance as a source of entertainment.

When we moved to Bauer, the car my parents bought included a radio. We would tune in to our favorite shows, especially as we drove home from a day of hiking or fishing. *The Jack Benny Show*, *Amos 'n' Andy*, *The Burns and Allen Show* and *Our Miss Brooks* sent us into peals of laughter. A joke-telling show featuring Joe E. Brown, Harry Hershfield and various guest raconteurs delighted us. I tried mightily to remember as many of the jokes as I could to regale classmates during lunch break at school. At home, though, our entertainment consisted mostly of reading, games, occasional conversation, and outdoor activities.

My parents had not brought the family radio with them in the move from Idaho to Utah, and my sister carefully guarded her Arvin in her room. Except for Saturday nights. That year, my sister brought her Arvin out of its seclusion.

She, my brother and I were often thrown on our own resources. Tooele lay too far from Bauer for us to reach it easily by bicycle, and the narrow highway we would have had to follow presented too much danger for us to risk it. In addition, we were not Mormon, and Tooele was a Mormon town, so none of the regular teenage evening social events would have included us, even if we could have managed to get there. Since we had to catch the bus home, we did not participate in whatever extracurricular activities the school may have offered. (I was invited to one all-school dance, and my date's father drove out to pick me up and return me home.) So we relied primarily on ourselves and each other for social life and entertainment.

On Saturday nights, at my insistent pleading, my sister would grant us the privilege of listening to the radio with her. The first time, she seemed to invite us into her room, but as soon as my brother and I had entered, she quickly stood, unplugged the set and carried it briskly out into the living room. She would not let us touch it or help in any way. Placing her prized possession on an end table, she found a socket, inserted the prongs and tuned the dial. Over the years, her interest in music had broadened to include country and western songs. As my brother and I leaned forward in silent anticipation, she would tune in the country music hit parade, broadcast from Clint, Texas.

In truth, I had not known my sister well since our intimate earliest years. From the time my brother entered school, my parents separated us three children into two categories: my sister and "the boys." I disliked that division intensely. I was barely a year younger than my sister, and almost two years older than my brother. Not only did I long for the privacy that my sister seemed to enjoy, I also missed the early, close connection she and I had developed. When my brother was still an infant and toddler, my sister and I had played and laughed together riotously. We made up games and invented languages. We danced and raced through the yard and house. We were constant and joyous companions. Our lives melded. But as my brother grew older, my parents insisted that I pair myself with him, and my sister faded from my view.

My sense of separation from my sister increased when, in our last year in Wallace, she suddenly left home and traveled halfway across the country to a Christian Science boarding school in Illinois for her ninth grade. At the time, I did not miss her much. My own life was filled with activities and the beginnings of adolescent sexuality and angst. But her empty room beckoned me, and I missed the sound of music from the Arvin radio on her desk. In my longing for a space of my own, I asked my mother if I could have her room while she was not using it. I received a peremptory "no." I also longed to reestablish my early childhood connection with my sister. I would sneak into her room to try to find a sense of that first intimacy.

In Bauer, again, my parents placed my brother and me together, using the house's fourth bedroom for storage, despite my protests. At the same time, my sister began to come into clearer focus for me. She seemed much more mature. Riding the train across the country by herself, finding her way in a new school, and managing missed connections in Chicago in a wild snowstorm over Christmas had given her a sense of confidence and courage she had not shown before.

During our year together as a family in Utah, my sister was a sophomore and I was a ninth-grader. In Tooele, junior high included the ninth grade. The high school and junior high occupied the same building, although with separate entrances. As first-year high school students, sophomores endured initiation rites during the second week of the school year. Relieved as I felt to be escaping those humiliations myself—we knew we would stay in Utah for only one year—I worried for my sister. When we descended from the bus on Monday of initiation week and she faced the gathered upperclassmen on the steps, who were jeering, taunting and threatening the sophomores as they tried to make their way up the gauntlet of the concrete stairway to the blocked front doors, I whispered, "Do you want me to sneak you in the junior high door?" She did not respond or glance at me. Gathering her books in her left arm, she braced her back, raised her head high, took a deep breath, strode across the walk and mounted the stairs, her right arm swinging, her eyes fixed straight ahead. As she ascended, the jeering faltered, then stopped, the taunts disappeared, the crowd silently parted, and she pushed through the doors without a backward or sideways glance. Then the din resumed.

She had done what I would not have had the courage to do. My love for her reappeared and increased. I sought time to talk to her at lunch. I tried to sit next to her on the bus. She still kept to herself; I still spent most of my spare time on weekends with my brother, but we did grow closer. Something shifted in me as I saw my sister make her way through that mob. As I was coming into my own maturity, I saw her as a new companion. Here and there, we began, tentatively, to talk about her experiences in boarding school, her classes, her ambitions and interests. Our original intimacy now formed the basis of a new, gradually growing closeness.

She introduced me to country music, a taste I have retained to this day. Clint, Texas, became an exotic, mythical place for my sister and me. I had no idea where it was or how the sounds could travel so far, so clearly over such a distance. I pictured them as waves, pulsing through the cold night air. Did the disc jockey realize that we teenagers in a distant settlement were huddled together, enchanted by the sounds he was broadcasting to us? No fiddling with the dial, no stringing the antenna to the roof; every nuance rang true. We heard Pee Wee Hunt sing "Send Me a Penny Postcard" in that high tenor of his. We thrilled to old Jimmie Rodgers recordings, and avidly memorized Hank Williams's lyrics. Patsy Montana entertained us, as did scores of others whose names I no longer recall.

The first blush of our teenage years, full of imagining and dreaming, resonated with that music. Popular songs of the day, such as "Red Sails in the Sunset" and "Slow Boat to China," had the same effect as they wafted from the car radio. I drifted away to distant places and compelling romance on those melodies. And from mysterious Clint,

Texas, floated the heartbreak of down-and-out, lost love and broken lives, with all the beautiful despair and vital hopelessness that burgeoning adolescence responds to. In the center of it all sits my sister's little, silver Arvin radio, singing and calling in the darkness of a lonesome Saturday night.

3

Not Kissing Carol Druby Good Night

"Did you kiss Carol Druby good night?" my mother stormed at me, her blue eyes aflame with rage. Her wrathful assault drove me back against the storm door I had barely closed, my hand still on the knob of the inside door.

"What?" I stammered, stunned and confused by the onslaught and by the question itself.

In late September of the year we lived in Bauer, my mother had organized a birthday party for my sister. This effort was out of the ordinary. Traditionally, we celebrated birthdays within the family; we did not include outsiders. Perhaps my mother wanted to make sure that my sister, fresh off her ninth-grade year at boarding school and now in a new town, to boot, would make friends. Whatever the reason, my sister invited a few new acquaintances from her classes, including Carol Druby, a girl in her grade who lived in Bauer and rode the bus with us to school in Tooele.

I don't recall that my father was home that evening; sometimes he stayed over in Salt Lake City, some forty-five miles away, where he was working that year.

My mother prepared cake and ice cream and hung a few decorations. Money was scarce that year, so we could not afford anything extravagant, much as that might have suited my mother's tastes. Parents drove the girls who lived in Tooele out to our house and arranged to pick them up a couple of hours later. These girls came dressed in colorful, patterned frocks, bright barrettes holding back their blond hair. They bore almost identical presents wrapped in striped pastel paper festooned with curly ribbons. Carol Druby, dressed more drably, walked down from her place five houses up the dirt road.

I paced the outskirts of the party. My mother had insisted that I attend, although I was the only boy present and had no idea of how to behave at a birthday party. In our family, though, we learned good social manners early, and my mother counted on that. It was also the beginning of a time, which would last through high school, when my mother commandingly enlisted my presence and activity in support of my sister's social life. Later on, it came to the point where she would insist that I accompany my sister to a formal dance, as her date, when she had not been invited by any other boy.

For this party, my mother organized and directed games, and circulated constantly to keep the conversation flowing. But the guests barely knew my sister, while they knew each other well, so they tended to fall back on chattering among themselves. The festive air my mother had hoped for never developed. My sister was clearly ill at ease as the gathering limped along toward its end.

I duly ate my portions of cake and ice cream, sang "Happy Birthday," and tried abortively to start a conversation with one or two of the guests. The other girls had no more idea why I was there than I did. My sister opened the presents and acted appreciative. The guests oohed and aahed appropriately.

Things finally perked up as parents began to arrive to retrieve their offspring. Relief, and with it a sudden, cheerful bonhomie, permeated the atmosphere. Uttering effusive thanks and assurances that they had had a wonderful time, the Tooele girls, fluttering like uncaged butterflies, flitted out the door and into the idling cars.

And there we were, the four of us: Carol, my mother, my sister and I. Carol seemed to be saying goodbye, too. My mother tried to detain her, but Carol pled the hour and parental rules. My sister hovered forlornly in the background. I stood by the door, waiting to release this last guest. But suddenly, when it became clear that Carol was, in fact, leaving, as she began to worm her arms into the sleeves of her coat, my mother decreed abruptly, "You will walk Carol home, Steve."

I expostulated, "But she only lives right up the road." I started to add, but quickly thought better of it, that she had managed to stroll down to our house solo in the darkening autumn evening and could just as well make it back up to her own house safely by herself.

"I raised you to be a gentleman, Steve," my mother replied sternly. "Gentlemen see ladies home." Carol had been ready to leave, her thank-you's concluded. Now she paused, uncertain. My mother looked at me steadily, her eyes making clear that she would brook no negotiation. Her left shoulder twitched microscopically. I dropped my eyes, stepped back out of the room, took from its hook in the hallway my light jacket against the late-September chill and slipped into it. I ushered Carol out the door gallantly. We descended the three concrete steps and proceeded down the frost-heaved front walk. I unfastened the metal gate, stood aside to let Carol pass and refastened the hasp behind us.

My fourteenth birthday was coming up in less than a month. Puberty had hit hard. A year or two before, my first erections had amazed and embarrassed me. They would occur by themselves, in public or private, with no prompting from me. I devised ways to hide them. If one sprouted up just as a teacher called on me to recite—those were the days when respect and decorum demanded that you rise and stand up straight when called upon—I would cleverly lift a textbook from my desk and hold it casually in front of my pelvis as I spoke. If I was walking down the corridor, I would mask the bulge with whatever I had in hand, bending over slightly until it subsided. Sitting seemed to provoke the most frequent of these discomfiting events, although they could occur at any time.

Wet dreams had also come into my life at that time. They starred a girl from school whom I knew only slightly.

Their violence and power disturbed and excited me. By the time we had moved to Bauer, however, my hormonal onslaught had abated somewhat. Random erections in public places rarely arose. My wet dreams had settled into a pattern of exciting, gratifying, if messy, sweetness that I happily anticipated at bedtime. A composite of female movie stars now acted the main role in my dreams, and the action, though vigorous, demanded more athleticism than violence.

That being said, shyness and inexperience, as well as implicit maternal prohibition, kept me from acting on my desires in any except the most tentative ways. Girls were beginning to take an interest in me, but I had little idea how to respond, and family strictures remained tight. There was a Hispanic girl in my Spanish class who would lean across the aisle, stroke my arms, look into my eyes and say, "Berry handsome, berry handsome." I imagined going off with her somewhere, perhaps to the woods outside of town, to engage in acts I had read about in *Sane Sex Life and Sane Sex Living,* the instructional book about intimate relationships that my mother had referred me to when I was nine or ten. In reality, though, I had no means to take her anywhere, and I quickly turned back to conjugating Spanish verbs.

Carol Druby and I started up the wide, dirt path between the road and the row of houses. We walked apart. We passed the place where, earlier that month, a giant bull snake had come boiling out of the brush in our overgrown yard, writhing almost across my feet. I had heard the rush of its body weaving and thrashing through the dry leaves and vines before it broke into view just in front of me. Its pale, thick body seemed to pass forever, thwacking little stones and twigs aside in its passage. It hissed loudly and aggressively, raising its head toward me as it whipped by. The prospect that it might swing back and attack terrified me.

I told Carol about it. She replied that she had seen such snakes, too, that they scared her, and that her father had killed one once. After that exchange, conversation faltered. We quickly reached her house. I drew the gate back for her chivalrously. We climbed the three chipped cement steps to her lighted side porch. As a gentleman, I needed to see her safely in. But she delayed opening the door, so we chatted briefly. The chill had increased, and I wanted to get home. The idea that she wanted me to kiss her good night did occur to me. The porch was tiny, a four-by-four concrete slab, so we were standing close together. She didn't attract me, and anyway, I wouldn't have known how to go about it if I had wanted to caress her. So I redirected the moment. I reached for the screen-door handle, opened the door part-way and thanked her for coming to the party. She pulled the door wide, twisted the inside knob and thanked me for walking her home. I said goodbye, hopped down the stairs and left.

I walked home through the dark autumn night, breathing the acrid smell of dry cottonwood leaves and arid earth, relieved by a duty scrupulously fulfilled, watching for bull snakes and eager to get to the warmth of my house and bed, with maybe another piece of birthday cake along the way.

Instead, I ran smack into the tornado of my mother's wrath. "Did you kiss Carol Druby good night?" she repeated, her voice raised and eyes flashing.

"No. Why would I?" I replied, stunned. What I didn't say was, "What business is it of yours, anyway?"

"Well, you certainly took your time walking her home," she challenged.

My sister hung in the background, looking the last thing like a birthday girl. Paper plates and cups lay strewn on the side table and on the arms of chairs, dollops of ice cream melting into crumbled pieces of cake and dripping over the sagging edges of the plates. Red Kool-Aid was beginning to soak through the sides of the cups. Wrapping paper and presents cluttered one corner.

"We talked for a minute on her porch," I explained, justifying myself as a matching anger rose unexpressed in my chest. "I went straight there and came straight back. I just walked her home, that's all." I barely refrained from bursting out with, "You're the one who told me to walk her home. I didn't want to. You ordered me to. And anyway, I didn't want to kiss her."

"Well, that better be all you did," she snapped suspiciously, "after the way she treated your sister." I looked across at my sister, still drooping there, but she offered no explanation. "As if it was *her* birthday, not your sister's," my mother barked. She paused briefly, as if still uncertain whether to believe me or not. Abruptly, she spun away, her rich alto voice switching from attack to command. "Well, let's get this cleaned up," she said briskly. "No, not you," to my sister. "It's your special day." My sister certainly didn't look like it was her special anything.

As I gathered up sticky plates, cups and utensils and carried them to the kitchen, my internal fury abated. I applied myself to the mundane task, relieved that my mother's attention had shifted away from me for the moment. But anger still roiled my mind. I had developed a romantic idea of kissing and sex. The transactional notion that you earned a good-night kiss from someone by behaving well at his sister's birthday party repelled me. Perhaps worst, my mother's coarse intrusion into my private, romantic sexual life felt incestuous and obscene.

As with all such events in our family, we did not process our feelings or even discuss them in any attempt to resolve the issue. My mother shut it down as absolutely as she had opened it up. I did not want to risk provoking another explosion by seeking an explanation, unfairly though she had treated me. My sister went to her room, I finished helping clean up and, without kissing anyone good night, ducked back into the room I shared with my brother, who had been absent from the whole brouhaha. Nobody ever spoke of the incident again, at least in my presence.

4

Mr. Bunn's Horses

Mr. Bunn kept three horses. Nick, Scrub, and Gypsy were their names, in descending order of size. My brother, sister and I, in ascending order of size, had never ridden before we moved to Bauer. But Mr. Bunn, the sole rancher in that tiny settlement, needed someone to exercise his horses, he said, and to reinforce their training. No one else in Bauer seemed willing or able, and there were three of us to match his three horses, so we took up the invitation as best we could.

In my early years, I had daydreamed of being a cowboy, as had almost every young boy, I suppose. But we had lived in logging and mining country, in mountains covered with evergreen forests, so my thought turned to being a forest ranger or a woodland explorer and mountain climber. Horses had slipped from my mind. All three of us children, now teenagers or almost, loved new challenges, though, so my early dreams re-arose.

I did not take to riding naturally. Large animals frightened me by their sheer size and my inability to read them accurately. But Mr. Bunn taught patiently and I began to grasp the rudiments. I even bought some rope and, under his amused but gentle tutelage, looped it into a lasso. I tried roping fence posts and tree stumps. Mr. Bunn taught me how to swing and throw the lasso.

He rode with us a few times, to begin with. Usually, he took my brother and me—my sister often had other activities. She participated in water ballet, in Tooele, and raced on the high school swim team. When Mr. Bunn took us out, he would ride Nick, with me perched on Scrub and my brother trailing on Gypsy. He favored Nick; he claimed the horse had an easy, strong walk that he could keep up all day. The other two had choppier gaits. And indeed, when we rode through the sage and brush on the hillsides behind the houses, Nick soon outdistanced the other two, and Mr. Bunn had to rein him in to let us catch up.

Mr. Bunn demonstrated how to halter the horses, bridle them and smooth the blankets over their backs before placing the saddles and cinching them. He watched us try and coached us until he thought we could do it well enough. He explained that the horses would sometimes take a deep breath and hold it while you fastened the cinch. As a result, the strap would loosen as you rode. That could prove dangerous; the saddle could slip sideways and roll you off. Nick, especially, could inflate his rib cage broadly and hold the air in while standing still. We learned to check each other's cinches after we had ridden away from the corral and the horses had begun to breathe deeply.

One time, the opposite happened. We weren't planning on a group ride; Mr. Bunn was simply trying out a new saddle. Scrub had been relaxing in his stall. Mr. Bunn saddled him in the barn, tightened the strap briskly and snugly, led the horse out, boosted my brother atop him and handed up the reins. My brother kicked him in the ribs, said, "Giddy-up," and leaned forward.

Scrub began to arch his back and hop in place. My brother paled, and Mr. Bunn stepped forward to grasp the bridle. Normally, Scrub obeyed without resistance or complaint. Now he tossed his head, then lowered it and bucked slightly. My brother grabbed the saddle horn. He kicked Scrub in the ribs again, but the horse refused the command. He continued to toss and snort in place.

Puzzled, Mr. Bunn circled him. It didn't seem as if he were trying to dislodge his rider, but his agitation grew. My brother held on gamely. After a moment or two of examination, Mr. Bunn figured out the problem. He loosened the girth a couple of notches and stood back. Scrub took a huge breath or two, chomped on the bit in relief and began a placid walk around the yard.

At the beginning of that year, my brother, sister and I lacked the skill and confidence to halter the horses readily. Their size and elusiveness daunted me. Without Mr. Bunn's help, we could easily spend the better part of a morning trying to catch them in the corral. Mr. Bunn, however, approached the horses without hesitation. He deftly and quickly looped the halters over their heads and led them to the rail, even Nick, the most recalcitrant of the three.

As my timidity lessened, however, I could usually, with persistence, catch and halter Scrub and Gypsy by myself, but Nick took at least two of us and long minutes. Even sugar cubes or apple slices might not entice him; he was too wily. I sometimes wondered, as I stood frustrated in the middle of the corral, the rough rope scratching my hand, if the extended effort was worth the pleasure of the ride, once we finally got to it.

At first, I could not manage to get comfortable in the saddle, let alone confident that I could control the horse. But Mr. Bunn showed himself to be a gentle, supportive and nonjudgmental teacher. His calmness and solid encouragement reassured me.

The rancher rode with ease, his tall, stocky body steady and in rhythm with Nick, as if he were just another part of the horse.

"Try sitting there like a sack of potatoes," he advised.

But I could rarely do that. My thin body, my sharp sit bones and the way my legs spread-eagled around the hard leather prevented ease most of the time. This was decades before I discovered the Buddhist meditative principle of being with what is. I fought the ache in my thighs and the pain in my sacrum. But once in a while, after long practice, I briefly achieved what he counseled.

One of those times, we were traversing the hillside above our house. The earth was soft, the horses ambled evenly, with Mr. Bunn slowing Nick down so we could all ride together. We were making our companionable way through the sage and dry grass and came upon the makeshift grave where my mother, brother and I had buried Sport, our dog. He had died the preceding fall, and the winter snow and wind had weathered our crude, wooden cross. But we could still make out the inscription in my handwriting.

Sport
The Best Dog in the World

Mr. Bunn glanced at the cross and asked, "Your dog?"

"Yes," I said.

He nodded, and we rode on. I felt grateful for his kind silence. I had feared he might consider the inscription too sentimental and scorn it. His nod of acceptance, with neither condolence nor further inquiry, touched me. His quietness opened space for my residual grief.

Mr. Bunn's kindness showed itself in other ways, too. He treated his young daughters with loving and careful attention. He showed respect and affection for his wife. He cared for his aging mother, who lived in the old ranch house outside the settlement.

He displayed overt impatience toward a person only one time in my presence. He had brought Gypsy down to the yard of the boardinghouse that Mrs. Bunn ran so that his daughters and his wife could pet her.

Gypsy stood patiently under the cottonwoods behind the building while Mr. Bunn set the girls in the saddle and let them hold the reins. She occasionally lowered her head to nip some grass. The girls squealed and laughed. Mr. Bunn chuckled, and Mrs. Bunn smiled.

A couple of other young children from nearby houses had joined the group, drawn by the festive air. A rambunctious girl, probably eight or nine years old, jumped up and down, asking loudly to ride the horse. She proclaimed that she had ridden before and knew how. Finally, Mr. Bunn acceded and hoisted her into the saddle.

All of his horses not only carried Western saddles, with horns and straps for lassos and sometimes holsters for rifles, they had also learned to respond only to neck reining, in the western tradition. Mr. Bunn's daughters had practiced laying a rein against Gypsy's neck on one side, and she had obediently turned her head to the other. Mr. Bunn asked this girl if she knew how to use the reins, to which she confidently answered, "Yes!"

But the second she had them in her hand, she separated them, taking one in each fist, and proceeded to yank the bit first left, then right, sawing Gypsy's mouth and shouting "Giddy-up!"

Mr. Bunn corrected her once, firmly, but in her blind enthusiasm, she paid no heed. Gypsy rolled her eyes, snorted and pawed the ground in confusion.

Uttering a sharp "Stop!" Mr. Bunn stripped the reins from her hands, seized her by the waist, unceremoniously swung her off and plopped her on the ground, hard. She stumbled as she righted herself.

Mr. Bunn's Horses

Mr. Bunn said sternly, "Don't ever treat one of my horses that way!" He drew a deep breath, and his sturdy shoulders relaxed as he stroked Gypsy's forelock.

That was the only time I saw him display harshness toward a human. Despite his general patience and good nature, however, he was a rough rancher who treated his animals without sentimentality. One day, he, my brother, and I had been for a ride and were unsaddling our mounts in the corral. I had freed Scrub and helped my brother take Gypsy's tack off, under Mr. Bunn's supervision. When Mr. Bunn had unsaddled and unbridled Nick, the horse continued to stand at the hitching rail, crowding Mr. Bunn and not joining his compatriots. Mr. Bunn swung his arm and drove the heel of his hand into Nick's flank, shouting "Go!" Nick flinched and veered away as Mr. Bunn shook his head and muttered something in irritation.

Besides his horses, Mr. Bunn had two dogs, one an old pet who spent her days lying on the ranch house porch, and the other a working dog who helped wrangle the ranch's cattle. One evening, I found Mr. Bunn standing by the big iron watering tank near the boardinghouse. He often brought the horses down to drink. I loved to watch their whiskered lips as they nosed down, then sucked up amazing amounts of the smelly liquid. Mr. Bunn said it didn't damage them, although we were forbidden to drink the same foul water that came out of the taps in our houses.

That evening, no horses drank. Mr. Bunn stood alone, peering out across the dry barrens at some cattle so far in the distance that they registered to my eyes as moving brown dots. At Mr. Bunn's feet lay his mottled, brown cow dog. The rancher gave a slight signal with his left hand, the dog leapt to its feet and made a beeline directly for the cattle, running at a speed I had never seen an animal attain before. Mr. Bunn's gaze continued to follow the dog's path as he became a spot at the head of a low haze of dust.

Suddenly, Mr. Bunn filled his lungs and gave a long, wavering whistle. The dog turned and the cattle began to move, first singly and then as a herd. In a few moments, he whistled again and the cattle changed directions slightly, the dog fast on their heels.

"What do the whistles do?" I asked.

"They tell him where to go and what to do," he responded, without looking at me.

"But it was the same whistle," I said, "and the cattle changed directions. How did he know how to do that?"

"It wasn't the same whistle. I gave him a different signal," he replied. "Didn't you hear the difference?"

I hadn't, and timidly acknowledged as much. He glanced at me and nodded. "They're all different. Listen." He whistled again and peered intently into the gathering dusk. I still couldn't distinguish one call from the other. In a few moments, he whistled yet a fourth time and turned his eyes away from the desert expanse.

"How do you know how to do that?" I asked, as a dark brown spot in the tan and gray landscape drew closer. I could barely whistle at all, despite my father's attempts to teach me. And even he had to put his fingers in his mouth to make such penetrating sounds.

"It takes training," he explained, "for him and for me. But it's worth it. It sure beats having to saddle up and spend a whole day rounding them up and moving them over."

That didn't sound like the cowboy way to me. Stories and songs had glamorized spending long hours in the saddle, driving cows. I had pictured "The Old Chisholm Trail" and "I'm Back in the Saddle Again." But here we were, standing at our ease and letting a dog do all the work. I did not say any of that; I respected Mr. Bunn too much and did not want to appear foolish in his eyes. I only later came to understand that people who do hard physical labor for a living appreciate anything that eases their burden a bit.

The dog raced back, past the watering tank, stopped at Mr. Bunn's feet, sat and looked up, his tongue lolling as he panted. Mr. Bunn looked down, said "Good" and gave another hand signal. The dog dashed away, up the road.

"Where are you sending him now?" I asked, since I knew of no cattle in that direction.

"Home," he said, "for the night. His work is done for now."

It seemed harsh to me not to have praised the dog more fully or to have petted him in appreciation for his work and obedience. That disturbed me. I didn't speak about it, but Mr. Bunn saw the look on my face.

"He's a working dog," he offered. "That's his job. You start petting him and praising him and he'll get lazy and stop obeying. That's his training, his life. You can't coddle him. We feed him, he sleeps in the barn, and he works. We have other dogs the girls can pet and play with. Not him; he's too valuable."

I thought of Sport, our English springer spaniel, whom we affectionately called Sporty. He had slept in a doghouse outside; my parents didn't allow him in the main house. But we played with him and hugged him and loved him. My father tried, sporadically, to train him to retrieve. Sometimes he would; other times he wouldn't. He was too much of a family pet. I figured Mr. Bunn was right, severe as it seemed to my young heart.

After that experience, I decided that my sister, brother and I should ride out, locate the cattle and see how hard it was, in fact, to move them a little. After some persuasion, they agreed. So, one sunny Saturday we walked up to the ranch and set about getting the horses ready.

For some mysterious reason, they complied obediently with our attempts to halter them and lead them to the hitching rail. Once there, they did not resist. I bridled and saddled Nick and helped my brother and sister with Scrub and Gypsy. We led the horses out, closed the corral gate, mounted and set off.

The horses settled into a walk, with Nick in the lead. As we left the cottonwood confines of the ranch, the desert spread out in front of us, drab and uninviting. Dust devils swirled in the distance. The late-morning sun scorched the landscape and heated the horses and us. I could see no cattle, but I led the way toward a rocky outcrop on a treeless mountain near where Mr. Bunn's dog had herded them.

As we progressed, the horses needed more and more urging. A headwind had sprung up and they tossed their heads. Nick's neck soon became wet to my touch, and a rim of white foam coated the front border of his saddle blanket. Bubbles of saliva blew from the ends of his bit.

After some time, we came to the point and rounded it. Another barren expanse opened to our view. I had hoped the outcrop might provide some shelter from the wind, where we could picnic. But we found only a jumble of small, jagged rocks, the hillside covered with low brush and the whole area windswept. I had no idea how cattle could survive there, although, evidently, they did. We saw desiccated droppings here and there.

I proposed we make the best of it, stop for lunch where we were and give the horses a rest. We dismounted stiffly and found some less uncomfortable places to sit on the stony ground. We put some rocks on the dangling reins to keep the horses from wandering off or leaving for home without us. But they seemed content to stay, snuffling and nibbling on the few withered plants within reach.

Despite the inhospitable surroundings, we remained in good spirits. We were out on the land, however arid, we all loved adventure, this was a new experience and, for once, the three of us had banded together without any adults. A sense of freedom, confidence and budding maturity infused us all. We laughed and talked as we ate our spam sandwiches, downed our V8 juice and sipped from our canteens.

As the sun tilted toward afternoon, we gathered up our few scraps, stowed them and agreed to head back. We spoke of exploring further, but decided against it. We could spy no cattle or greenery in any direction except the now remote dusty trees around the ranch and in Bauer. We stroked the patient horses, freed their reins and mounted, me boosting my brother onto Scrub.

On the way out, despite our diligent efforts, clucking and leaning forward, as Mr. Bunn had taught us, and digging our heels into their sides, all three horses had refused to break into a trot, let alone a lope or gallop. We had eventually settled for Nick's fast walk, with Gypsy and Scrub trotting briefly to catch up. In my innocence, I had expected the same recalcitrance on the ride back.

Was I ever wrong! No sooner had I turned Nick's head than he snorted and strode out in his swiftest walk toward the speck that was the ranch. The wind at his rump, he covered the ground at a pace I would have had to jog to match. Gypsy, and then Scrub, broke into a trot to keep up. The staccato clop of their hooves on the stony ground excited Nick. He picked up his gait, too.

We had always longed for the excitement of racing along, but Mr. Bunn had frequently cautioned us against it. He feared we might be thrown, or exhaust and injure the horses in our exhilaration. So I leaned back in the saddle and hauled on the reins, with momentary success. I also wanted to extend the outing with my brother and sister, but the horses were of a different mind. They fed off each other and increased their pace. I still had not learned to ride a trotting horse with skill or ease. I jolted from sacrum to skull at that gait, as did all of us. Surrendering, we gave them their heads. And once we had set them loose, we no longer had control. Off they sped.

Holding Nick's reins between the fingers of my left hand, I tried, with sporadic success, to avoid seizing the saddle horn. To my right, my brother clung to Scrub with all his boyhood might. And far out on my left, I saw Gypsy outstrip us both. Her head and neck extended far forward, she ran low to the ground. I could barely make out the earth beneath her belly. Her forehooves reached and pulled, her hind hooves pushed and stretched. Her black mane waved like a banner, her tail a pennant.

And my sister! Crouched over the saddle, her blond hair a blur, she had become one with her horse. The reins hung loose in her left hand, her right hand swung wide and free, floating with the rhythm of the animal beneath her. Focus and joy marked her profile.

I had come to admire my sister that year, for her grit and determination, qualities I had not noticed so clearly or respected so deeply before. Seeing her that afternoon, wild and sure and purely herself, added another dimension to my honoring her.

We arrived at the corral in less than half the time it had taken us to go out. The lathered horses, their sides heaving, slowed to a walk when we reached the cottonwoods. They eased to the corral gate, where Mr. Bunn met us. He had kept an eye on us, even as he did his chores.

He nodded with approval at me, as the leader of the expedition. He praised my brother, the youngest. For my sister, he saved a special smile and warm greeting as she led

Gypsy to the hitching rail. He helped us stow the gear, then instructed us in wiping down the horses and cooling them before we released them to their feed and water.

That ride took place in the middle of August. Within a few days, our family left, as planned, and moved to southern Nevada for my father's work. I rode horses a few times after that, on separate occasions. I say I rode them; I sat upon them as they went along. I recalled Mr. Bunn's teachings and did the best I could. The intimate relationship I had had with Nick and Scrub, and even Gypsy, whom I never rode, did not return.

I remember to this day the smell of Nick's sweat, the cut in his left ear that gave him his name, the way his huge body moved. I remember Scrub's hoarse breathing as he worked uphill. Somewhere in my storage room still hangs the lasso Mr. Bunn taught me to make that year. Vivid in my aging mind glows the sight of my sister, flying free with Gypsy for those long minutes in her all-too-short life. And gratitude rises in my heart to Mr. Bunn for taking us under his wing, for his kind instruction, for his acceptance and for introducing us to Gypsy, Scrub and Nick.

5

Oatmeal, Not Black-Eyed Peas

Once, we lived on oatmeal for a week: three meals a day for
my mother, two for us children, who had lunch at school,
and my father, who ate at work. For the first two days, milk
and sugar made it palatable. On the third morning, the milk
ran out, and that evening we shook the last few grains from
the sugar bag into our gelatinous bowls.

We eked by that year when we lived in Bauer. Major transi-
tions defined our lives. My father had lost his job in northern
Idaho the preceding spring, when he was in his late forties,
and had accepted a new one that required a year of training
at a token salary. My sister and I had hit early adolescence,
and my brother was creeping up on it. Riding a bus, which
we had not had to do before, to and from a new school in a
different town, deprived us of the chance to participate in
after-school activities, such as they might have been. Aware
that we would be leaving in a year, anyway, we hesitated to
form the close friendships we might otherwise have prized.

My mother suffered the most that year, I think, although she rarely complained. Formerly active in church and community organizations, she found no outlet for her talents and interests. Bauer offered minimal social life and no amenities whatsoever, and Tooele was an almost exclusively Mormon town, while we actively practiced Christian Science. Friendly and sociable woman that she was, she drifted on her own much of the time.

My father traveled to Salt Lake City on weekdays and worked long hours. He enjoyed his job and the professional companionship it offered, things my mother's life lacked. He mentioned more than once an evening invitation that he had declined with regret because he needed to catch the bus home to Bauer. That year, both of them missed the social interactions they had valued and thrived on in the past. Knowing the circumstances were temporary helped sustain my mother's occasionally flagging spirits somewhat, although our reduced financial circumstances created a constant strain for her, especially since she managed the family budget.

I did not like oatmeal to begin with. When I was a younger boy, its slimy texture had stimulated the beginning of a gag response in me. Liberal doses of brown sugar, a handful of raisins, and just enough whole milk to soften the glop made it tolerable. I preferred almost any other hot cereal. My dislike had lessened over the years, but not disappeared.

All the same, something in my character gravitated toward endurance. I had thrived on rationing during World War II. More than just the idea of contributing to the war effort drew me. I had read about the Native American practice of taking only what you need from the land and water, and had adopted that attitude as my own without formulating it.

When rationing ended, my father urged me to eat butter, but I refused. The idea of such indulgence and excess offended my boyhood sensibilities. My thin frame and firm beliefs survived, and thrived, on some burgeoning sense of the importance of self-discipline for my own and the greater good.

Surviving for a week primarily on oatmeal came as no deprivation; rather, as an opportunity. I embraced it. I understood that finances had grown tight. Providentially, we had a large tub of cereal. Compassion for my father, who could not provide as he would have liked to, and a desire to support the whole family, combined with my native attraction to minimalism, dominated my feelings.

I watched the level of oatmeal sink as the week wore on, and estimated how long the supply would last. I began to entertain the notion of quitting school and going to work in the mine, an impractical step for me at the age of fourteen, but self-sacrifice appealed to me, as did my vision of the family's appreciation and respect.

I proposed the idea to my mother, but she snapped, "That's not your job. It's your father's. He's supposed to get a check on Friday, and I'll buy us real food on Saturday morning. Your job is to study. Go do it." Which I did.

Saturday morning, we ate the last of our oatmeal and my mother headed to town. I had anticipated a happy, celebratory lunch of our usual fare, but covert discord reigned. My mother's grievance with my father for our predicament had soured their interactions. His sullen silence clouded the atmosphere. Her defiant cheer as we brought in the bagsful of groceries from the car tightened the tension, rather than dispelling it.

The lunch she laid out with such apparent gaiety disturbed and puzzled me. Potato chips, pickles, relishes, sliced head cheese, liver sausage, snacks of all sorts and special breads and crackers covered the bare table. No staples such as we normally ate appeared.

"I know you've been worried," she announced, "so now let's forget about that and have some treats, splurge a little." She began urging these unfamiliar delicacies on us.

I glanced at my father on my left. He was sitting at the head of the table, restrained anger registering on his face. He taciturnly accepted the servings my mother passed him and began to chew, his cheeks and nose reddening. His jaws worked methodically, the muscles bunching and stretching.

My parents had taught us to chew with our mouths closed, and they modeled it. A boyhood hunting accident, which led to a surgeon removing parts of my father's intestinal tract, forced him to masticate his food long and thoroughly before swallowing. That noontime, he pulverized his nourishment even more slowly than usual, his right cheek puffed with cud, his heavy breathing audible through his stress-swollen nostrils. An uneasy silence settled over the meal. My mother's forced chatter subsided.

Financial issues plagued my parents. My father, although he grew up an only child, doted upon by his mother, became frugal, even miserly. He fretted about spending, especially that year. My mother, in contrast, spoiled by her half brothers and indulged by her father in girlhood, developed a cavalier attitude toward money. Splurges excited and gratified her. Her father descended from a long line of Germans, whom delicatessen (*delikatessen*) fare both reassured and comforted. For my mother, that lunch returned her to the safety and community of her childhood. For my father, who bore little respect for his father-in-law to begin with, it represented heedless excess and looming ruin.

So my father chewed, his stifled emotional stew overheating the emulsion in his mouth. My mother, her initial urgings having abated, relapsed into filling her own plate repeatedly and uttering unpersuasive sounds of pleasure between mouthfuls.

My sister ate little; she absented herself from the family as much as she could that year and often sought the seclusion of her room. My brother helped himself generously; he ate heartily and managed to block out most of the tension in the family when he was a boy. I sat nervously, ever attuned to discord between my parents, sparingly forking small bites into my mouth.

When I helped clean up, leftovers of everything littered the counters—bits and remnants and half-full jars and cans that we somehow piled into the refrigerator. Some we snacked on over the next week; some we eventually had to discard as waste. None of that assortment ever sufficed for another meal.

After that failed pageant, we settled back to more stable nutrition. One Friday evening, my mother brought home a large sack of black-eyed peas she had found on sale. She admitted that she had never eaten or cooked black-eyed peas, and had no recipe for them, but reckoned you just boiled them the way you did pinto or kidney beans. She said we needed to try new things.

Saturday morning, she dug out a large pot, filled it with water, tossed in a handful of table salt and set several cups of peas to simmering. The odor when she lifted the lid to check if they had softened yet drove me from the room and eventually outdoors. To say it was unappetizing minimizes the smell's effect on me. I roamed the hill behind the house to clear my head and settle my stomach, target practicing with my Red Rider BB gun until my mother sent my brother to call me in around midday.

Those black-eyed peas comprised the main dish at lunch. My mother ladled out a large, steaming dollop on each of our plates, with a wedge of iceberg lettuce on the side. I tried; I did. I was a dutiful son. Holding my breath, I hesitantly raised a small forkful to my mouth and took a single chew. I began to retch, spit the wad into my left palm and dumped it back on the plate. I quickly downed a gulp of Kool-Aid and bit off a chunk of lettuce.

"Don't you like it?" my father asked, his cheek abulge.

"I'm sorry," I said. "I can't help it. It's just . . . the taste makes me feel sick to my stomach and I don't want to vomit."

"Have you been feeling sick today?" he pursued the discussion.

"No," I replied. "I've been fine. It's just that taste."

"Well, it is unusual," he continued, masticating for a few seconds and looking at the ceiling thoughtfully. "But not bad," he said, looking the length of the table at my mother. "Maybe if you just give it another try and start slowly. Mix it in with some lettuce until you get used to it."

"I can't," I replied. "I don't want to upset the meal. But I like the lettuce," I added, crunching off another piece. I tried to sound convincing and conciliatory.

"Well, that's what's for lunch," my mother announced sharply. "And I bought a big chocolate cake with lots of frosting for dessert. If you don't eat your black-eyed peas, you won't have any chocolate cake."

She had never issued such an ultimatum before, to any of us. I looked briefly at her distressed, flushed face, glanced down at my plate with its cooling heap of legumes, then met her eyes again and nodded.

"I hope you understand," she rapped out. "No black-eyed peas, no chocolate cake."

"I understand, mother," I said calmly. I returned to my plate and tucked into the remaining lettuce. I realized that our uncertain financial situation and relative social isolation that year had pushed my mother to an emotional edge and that my rejection of her attempt to nourish her family had stung her deeply. I had never before refused her cooking, so the punishment seemed just to my mind.

More than empathy drove my behavior, however. My adolescent mind also grasped absolute dictates. I had been raised on firm discipline to begin with, and this bargain, radically out of character though it was, struck me as fair. I embraced it. My mother's steady glare gave me to know that she expected me to cave. But adherence to principle, an inclination toward heroic deprivation and a valorous endurance prevailed.

My father endeavored to soften the moment, as my siblings sat in silence. "Just give it another try," he nudged me gently. "Maybe you'll get used to the taste. It's good." He nodded at my mother to let her know that he would not try to countermand her finality.

I impaled two peas on one tine of my fork, raised the implement halfway, shook my head as my stomach churned, lowered my hand and scraped the peas off on the rim of my plate, wiped the prongs of my fork on my paper napkin and returned to the remains of my lettuce. I ate the lettuce like a starving rabbit. When I asked for another wedge, my mother graciously granted my request, sure I would eventually falter.

When everyone except me had cleaned their plates, my mother rose, opened the cupboard and produced a giant, three-layer, Betty Crocker chocolate cake slathered with thick frosting. With a flourish, she placed it in the middle of the table, produced a long, slender knife from a drawer and, with a sweet smile, inquired who wanted a piece.

Without my father saying anything, my mother sliced a double piece and asked me to pass it to him. My sister received a small slice—she was watching her weight. My mother doled out a substantial portion to my brother and took a similar one for herself. She looked at my plate, shook her head, seated herself and said gaily, "Now we can dig into this treat." She moved a large forkful to her mouth and sighed enthusiastically.

In my family, you did not leave the table until everyone had finished eating, my mother had declared the meal to be over, and had pushed back her chair and risen. I sat, watching the mound of black-eyed peas congeal under my nose. The sugary, buttery aroma of store-bought cake drifted around the small kitchen.

Years later, when I was living in Ithaca, New York, the memory of that lunch came back to me and I searched out recipes for black-eyed peas. I found one called Hoppin' John. You diced a white onion, cubed a substantial slab of salt pork, sprinkled the combination with some black pepper, sautéed it lightly in butter and added it to the simmering peas when they were just getting soft. I loved the dish and made it often for myself and friends. But that was decades later.

That noontime in Bauer, I stuck to my guns. My father essayed one more time to persuade me, but my adamantine convictions held. I would endure my punishment. If that was the bargain, that was the bargain. Enticing though the cake smelled, and slowly though the others were savoring it, a deal was a deal. I'd made my choice and, by golly—we didn't swear in my family—I'd hold to it. Expanding my thin torso, I drew in a deep, victorious breath.

Halfway through dessert, my mother capitulated. "Well," she said to my father, "I guess he's learned his lesson. And maybe I was too harsh and spoke in the heat of the moment." She turned to me. "Here, pass me your plate. I'll clean it off and give you some cake."

The prospect tempted me, and I wavered momentarily. But something more important ruled my response, something to do with my own integrity. "No, thank you," I said.

My parents both leapt in with "It's alright, you tried, you can have some," while my brother stared enviously at the substantial helping I might get.

"No, thank you," I repeated. "I really don't want any."

Back and forth we went for a bit, until my mother broke it off and said, "Fine, I guess lunch is over," and stood up abruptly. I knew her anger resulted from my intransigence, even after she had relented. I knew she loved me and regretted her earlier words. But in my life so far, my mother had preached inviolable standards. I had determined to live by them, and, in that moment, to force her to, as well. And I had just turned fourteen, with all the subtle emotional cruelty that age can involve. We cleaned up and went our separate ways.

I don't remember what we had for supper that night. Not black-eyed peas. I cleaned my plate with gusto. For dessert, we delighted in the rest of the cake. I ate my piece without quibble, slowly savoring its softness and flavor. It was good.

August 1950

The author (right) stands with his brother and sister
in front of a sign at the Bonneville Salt Flats Speedway,
shortly after the family's arrival in nearby Bauer.

The author fires a .22 rifle while his mother,
sister, and brother look on.

Fall   1948

The author's mother fires the .22 rifle
while Sport the dog looks on.

The author (left) stands with his mother, sister, and
brother in August 1950, shortly after arriving in Bauer.

The author's father, a few years before
the family moved to Bauer.

Sport the dog in 1941, nine or so years
before the family moved to Bauer.

6

Setting Mr. Perks's Lawn on Fire

My brother and I set fire to Mr. Perks's lawn. More exactly, to the twigs and leaves on the lawn. The dry grass—what there was of it—survived, scorched here and there. We did it inadvertently, though dramatically.

Cottonwood trees lined the decrepit, wire-mesh fence between Mr. Perks's house and ours. That day, I had been walking up the dirt road from the guppy pond, where I had been checking on the sunken boat we had resurrected earlier. I was wool-gathering in the sun's warmth as I ambled. When I opened our front gate, my brother interrupted my reverie by calling excitedly to me from our driveway. His demeanor struck me. He rarely showed such enthusiasm and even more rarely invited me to share one of his activities. He urged me to come look at something.

I had been headed inside, filled with my own thoughts, and I didn't want to be sidetracked. But he insisted so eagerly that I acceded and changed directions, expecting something mundane or a trick of the kind he often tried to play. He frequently delighted in leading me to agree to some bargain and, after I had kept my side of it, going back on his part by arguing a technicality. (As an adult, he eventually became a lawyer.) So I approached warily. He was standing on a broken section of cement under the cottonwoods. An open box of wooden matches lay on the ground beside him.

"Look!" he exclaimed. He bent and gathered a handful of the cotton that had drifted down from the trees. He extracted a match from the box, struck it on the concrete and held the flame to the edge of the pile. The pile vanished.

"See," he exclaimed, as if he were Thomas Edison showing off his light bulb. "It doesn't even burn. It just disappears."

"It has to burn," I objected, peering down. "It must be that the fluff is so light it burns too fast for you to see the flames."

"No, no," he argued. "The ground under it doesn't even get hot." He patted where the cotton had lain. "You try it," he pressed me. "You'll see."

I hesitated, demurred, looking for the catch. Playing with fire had never attracted me, and I didn't trust his motives. Seeing my reluctance, he gathered another, larger mound and lit it. Momentarily, I saw a quick flick of flame as this heap, too, vanished.

More to humor him than anything else—I wanted to be on my way and still felt suspicious—I knelt, gathered a substantial bunch and put a match to it. It melted away with an almost invisible flare of fire. Doing it myself changed my mood, and the apparent magic of it engaged me. I gave up and joined his excitement.

Snowbanks of cotton edged the driveway, the fence and the bases of the corrugated tree trunks. Ranging farther afield, we gathered more and more as new material floated from the limbs and coated the ground. Cautioning my brother to follow my lead, I made sure to clear the burn area of any other fuel around our gatherings. At first, we did that scrupulously, laughing and remarking together. But then, feeding off each other's building energy, we grew careless. My brother tried igniting a clump that had clung together by itself beside one of the trees. The cotton evaporated, but with tiny, orange flares visible. Instantaneously, neighboring accumulations disappeared and low puffs of smoke arose as the heat consumed the white covering nearer and nearer the fence.

Suddenly alarmed, we attempted to stomp it out, but we could not discern where it was headed. I dashed into the house, grabbed a broom and started sweeping the tinder away from the fence, onto the driveway. We kicked at what we could see and strove to get ahead of the barely visible conflagration. But the white blanket spread in all directions and was melting away like cotton candy in a child's mouth.

"I'll get the hose," I yelled and raced to the spigot on the outside of our house. The hose, which we had never used, had long since been disconnected. I grabbed the attachment dangling from the rack. The ancient rubber crackled as I tugged. It broke, and the end came off in my hand.

Too late, anyway. I sped back, only to see the cotton melting away through the fence and onto Mr. Perks's lawn. Frantically, we hoisted ourselves over the sagging wire mesh and tried, with our feet and hands, to make a firebreak of bare ground. But we could not tell where to work. By now, the low-lying wildfire had spread beyond our control. It was a secretive, fleet fire.

More bursts of smoke had begun to arise, and the acrid smell of burning twigs and detritus assailed my nostrils. The fire had now reached the banks of unraked leaves blown against the cinder block foundation and under the splintered siding of Mr. Perks's house. Random flames were licking the dry wood and peeling paint. Visions of Mr. Perks's house, and all the other dried-out, wooden houses along that side of the road, exploding into flame overwhelmed my imagination with pictures of courtrooms and jails.

Desperate now, and looking around wildly, I spied a newer-looking, green hose coiled on the ground and attached to a pipe projecting from the back of Mr. Perks' house. Heedless of the burning lawn, I hopped across it, twisted the handle and began to shoot sulfur-smelling water all around the foundation of the house, shouting to my brother to get help.

It was about this time that Mr. Perks himself came strolling up the road from the plant, looking around at this and that, turned in and opened the low metal gate to his front walk. He was peacefully coming home for a leisurely lunch. In our alarm and efforts, we had not heard the noon whistle.

Mr. Perks stood about five-foot-four. His formerly red hair was fading, thinning and receding. It lay in strands on his pale scalp. His freckled, homely face glistened with perspiration. His chubby body moved clumsily. He lived alone and seemed in some ways like an outcast. But he was one of the few who had taken a supportive interest in our boating project and usually had a cheerful word to say. Our interactions held a sincere and friendly tone. So I was especially ashamed that it was his house we were endangering.

He closed the gate, raised his head and noticed us, as I sprayed and my brother sought to contain the outbreaks on the lawn. Mr. Perks observed us for a moment or two and then said calmly, "Got a fire there, boys?"

I apologized madly, explaining in staccato bursts what had happened as I played the nozzle around, soaking everything the water would reach. I omitted the part about us intentionally setting fires, hoping he wouldn't glance through the fence and see the box of matches still lying there. I did my best to make it sound like an unfortunate accident, which, in a way, it was. Mr. Perks surveyed the scene with no apparent concern on his ruddy, splotched face, nodded, turned and walked up onto his porch and into his house.

By now, things had begun to settle down a bit. I circled the house as far as the hose would stretch, dousing any remaining smoke puffs. The fire had not spread to the front or far side. It had remained in the near side and backyard where the cotton was thickest. Beyond that, it ran out of fuel. The heat had seared the lawn in patches, leaving small, brown, irregular shapes. But the house had not burned— nor had we.

My brother and I had stopped shouting to each other. We worked silently. I turned the hose off and re-coiled it carefully. Then, with one more thorough look, we slunk stealthily back over the fence. My brother surreptitiously placed the matches where they belonged, in a kitchen drawer. We went our separate ways and said no more about it. Chastened, we did not mention it to our parents, nor did we practice to be juvenile arsonists again.

I had feared the incident would strain our neighborly relationship with Mr. Perks, but the opposite happened. It was as if our setting fire to his yard, and nearly to his house, had broken the ice and initiated even more cordial interactions. I was embarrassed to see him after that event, but he evidently held no ill will. Quite the contrary, in fact.

Mr. Perks was the first one in the settlement that I knew of to own a television set. In towns and cities, they may already have gained popularity. But Bauer did not lie on the cutting edge of popular culture, and we did not even own a family radio that year, let alone anything fancier and more modern.

One noontime, shortly after we had enflamed his yard, Mr. Perks saw my brother and me playing basketball at a netless hoop on the dirt pathway along the road. He passed his gate and waddled toward us, a smile on his chubby face. "Come in, boys. I've got something I want to show you."

Seeing us hesitate, he added, "I've got a TV. Brand new. Have you ever watched TV?" We hadn't. I had heard of television, but had never seen a set, let alone watched a program. Since my brother and I were together, accepting his invitation seemed safe enough, despite my mother's life-long caution not to go into strangers' houses. Besides, Mr.

Setting Mr. Perks's Lawn on Fire

Perks was no longer a complete stranger to us, and he was displaying a childlike pleasure and innocent excitement. In we went. The living room smelled fusty. Heavy curtains covered all the windows. No other humans greeted us, and no pets appeared. The few pieces of furniture I could dimly make out appeared unused and dingy. He led us to the kitchen, where sunlight filtered in through dusty panes of glass. A large, box-like apparatus sat on one end of a Formica table. He pointed to the object with beaming pride.

I estimated that the dark screen, set in the middle of a large, silver housing, measured about eight inches by twelve inches. Several dials jutted from the bottom of the frame. Mr. Perks twisted one of them, saying, "Now watch this." He stood back and we waited, I wasn't sure for what. A long wire extended from the back of the set and out the window. A black cord ran to an outlet indented in the floor directly under the table.

As we waited, the set now emitting a low hum, I inquired about the wire. He said it was the antenna. He added that there were things called "rabbit ears" that would help with reception. He planned to buy some next time he got to town, and connect them.

The screen blinked a few times, flashed and started to glow. Turning up the volume, he fiddled with another knob to find the channel he wanted. (This was well before cable TV or remote controls.) Static filled the room and snow blanketed the screen. As he tuned, human-like figures began to appear amid the blizzard. I shifted from one foot to the other; the air in the kitchen was close and stale.

Timidly, I asked him what we were watching.

"Wrestling," he said. "Women's wrestling. They really go at it." He adjusted the focus some more. "You'll see," he added ebulliently. And indeed, I did begin to make out muscular, vaguely female figures banging into each other, clinging, separating, lunging, falling. A loud male voice, barely intelligible, kept up a rapid, almost hysterical, narration of the action.

But the static began to hurt my ears as he dialed the volume up to try to catch the announcer's words, and swirling flakes prevented me from making out anything clearly. I soon found myself bored, despite Mr. Perks's enthusiasm, and shifted my eyes right and left, seeking a path of escape. I itched to be outside again, away from the din and glare. I began to edge toward the door. My brother continued to stare raptly.

Mr. Perks endeavored to detain me. He insisted that I would be enthralled. He wanted me to share his delight and didn't understand my desire to flee. But I persisted as I backed away. I politely thanked him and said we had to leave, pleading our own lunchtime. My brother stood engrossed. Only after I tapped him on the shoulder and nodded toward the door did he reluctantly follow me, turning back to glance at the wavering screen several times.

As I squinted my way through the darkened living room, Mr. Perks called after us, "And I'm going to get an antenna for the roof. You can come watch anytime." I called my thanks to him again, and we made our way out.

Setting Mr. Perks's Lawn on Fire

That episode caused me to realize how lonely Mr. Perks must have been. I suspected that he did not easily make friends with his colleagues at the plant. I never saw him with any coworkers or neighbors. No other cars came to park in front of his house. And little in Bauer connected us to the larger outside world. Without a female companion, he must have felt all the more bereft. He may have found women's wrestling, with the scanty costumes and physical contact, particularly alluring.

I never took him up on his invitation, although he occasionally renewed it. Despite my own burgeoning puberty and growing interest in girls, the prospect of watching women's wrestling had failed to entice me. All the same, my friendly interactions with Mr. Perks continued for the rest of my family's stay in Bauer. We chatted when we met. Once or twice, when I noticed that his yard had become especially desiccated and dusty, I climbed openly over the fence, turned on his hose and watered his lawn copiously.

7

Why I Did Not Become an Eagle Scout but How I Did Get Invited to the Ninth-Grade Prom

Dennis Long invited me to become an Eagle Scout. He and I had grown to be daytime friends. Riding the bus immediately to and from school limited the friendships my brother, sister and I could develop. Still, we did get to know some of our peers fairly well and would chat with them between classes. During lunch break, students congregated in the building or in the schoolyard, so we had some time to become well acquainted with one or two of them.

Like me, Dennis was a ninth-grader, and we shared several classes. We sat next to each other and solved algebra problems together. He lived in Tooele, but ate lunch at the school cafeteria, where we often sat together. He took a shine to me and we began to seek each other out.

As winter turned to spring, he began to talk excitedly about his scout troop. He told me proudly that he had achieved the rank of Eagle Scout. He spoke enthusiastically about the pending pack trip into the High Uintas his troop was planning for the summer. I had grown up camping with my family, and we exchanged stories, although it turned out that I had experienced far more of the outdoors than he.

Then one day, as we stood in the crowded yard waiting for the bell to ring, he asked me if I would like to join his troop. His question took me aback momentarily. I had been a Cub Scout years before, but had not continued with the activity. The idea that I could become an Eagle Scout without going through any of the preceding steps baffled me.

When I questioned Dennis about it, though, he assured me that they would welcome me. They were seeking new members my age. He was confident I would fit in and easily pass the requirements, about which he spoke vaguely and uncertainly.

The prospect of a backpacking trip into the High Uintas allured me. Circumstances had forced our family to stop camping a few years earlier, and I missed it sorely. The bleakness of the desert around Tooele increased my longing for clear-running water and forested mountains. I actually had no idea where, exactly, the Uintas were or what kind of terrain they contained. Our family had picnicked up a canyon in the Wasatch Mountains when we first came to Utah. I built a picture of the mysterious Uintas on that memory.

I spoke to my parents about Dennis's proposal. My mother enthusiastically supported the idea. She had been my den mother in the Cub Scouts and believed in the value of belonging to worthy organizations. She also wanted me to break out of my artistic and scholarly shell and grow up to be a "man's man," as she termed it. My father nodded in agreement, although he expressed regret that he could not take me himself. So I let Dennis know, and he happily agreed to consult with the scoutmaster and set a date for my introduction to the troop and senior scouting. My mother offered to drive me into Tooele and pick me up on the appointed evening.

About the same time as this was happening, I began to notice that girls were taking an interest in me. In fact, they may have been for some while. I was a shy boy and, despite my burgeoning fantasies of romance, tended to keep to myself. My interactions with girls had ranged from awkwardness to avoidance. But pubescence had hit hard and piqued my interest and curiosity.

A few girls flirted with me in classes and in the hallways. I usually realized what they had done only in retrospect. I tried to focus on my schoolwork, and my mother's moralistic prohibitions against treating women with anything but the utmost respect constantly loomed in my mind. Competing forces battled within me. My sexual urges and native romantic vision struggled, for the most part vainly, to break free from maternal strictures.

In the winter, when harsh weather confined us to the school building during lunch hour, eager teenage bodies packed the corridors. Hissing metal radiators exuded steam heat. A few of the older couples paired off to talk intimately; the rest of us roamed.

Why I Did Not Become an Eagle Scout

Girls from my class occasionally bumped into me "accidentally" and apologized with a toss of their hair and a quick, direct glance. At a loss for how to start a conversation, I would mutter something like "That's okay" and move on. Once or twice, I returned the glance and held it, but the possibilities I imagined struck me dumb.

Dennis and I set a date and time for me to come to my first scout meeting. Dennis told me he had spoken to the scoutmaster and received permission for me to join. He assured me that everyone would greet me gladly, but something in his manner struck me as evasive. He did meet my gaze when I asked him if it truly was okay, since I had no previous experience with senior levels of scouting. His soft, brown eyes shifted away and down, his feet shuffled, and his sloping shoulders drooped. But in my eagerness, I wrote it off as part of the newness of the idea.

My mother drove me into town on the appointed evening and dropped me off early near the Mormon church building, adjacent to the school grounds, where Dennis stood waiting. He had told me the hourlong meeting was to start at seven, and she planned to pick me up at eight. She called a grateful greeting to Dennis, smiled at me and drove off.

May had arrived, and the school year was nearing its end. Members of the ninth-grade class were growing excited, and not just for summer vacation. Junior high in Tooele ran from seventh through ninth grade. We could look forward not only to a graduation ceremony but also to a class prom the week before we received our diplomas.

I had never been to an actual dance. The year before, I had attended a "dance" that included eight students and some instruction in basic ballroom steps. The small, brightly lit room provided no sense of intimacy, and the chaperone required us to change partners after every number she played on the small record player in the corner. So I paid little attention to the growing chatter about the prom in the hallways and schoolyard. The end-of-year exams absorbed me.

Students called the prom a "reverse." (In other places, such an event would be called a "Sadie Hawkins.") Girls invited boys. One noontime, out in the schoolyard, a girl from my grade, named Zoe Ann Rutledge, approached me. She walked directly up to me, called my name, stopped face to face and asked, "Will you go to the ninth-grade prom with me?" Her mahogany eyes shone as her full lips moved. A few strands of her chestnut hair, combed at an angle across her brow, fluttered in the slight breeze.

Perhaps it was her boldness that generated a matching daring in me. Without stepping back from her close proximity, I said, "Yes, I would like to." I hoped my breath did not waft the odor of the stewed tomatoes the cafeteria had served for lunch. Hers smelled faintly of Dentyne chewing gum.

Her cheeks dimpled. We did not move, two adults for the moment. Then I bethought myself as she looked up at me. "I'll need to ask my parents if I can go," I added.

She nodded. "I already asked mine. You can tell me tomorrow."

I hesitated. "How will I find you?" The lawn and building teemed with students and faculty, and I had not really noticed her closely before. As far as I could remember, we had not spoken.

"I'll find you," she replied. "You're tall and I'll recognize you. Just wait here after lunch. I go home for lunch; I live right over there." She pointed to an adjoining street. She nodded again, said, "See you tomorrow," and walked toward the building, her hips swaying slightly as she went. I had a hard time concentrating on my afternoon studies.

I walked quickly up to Dennis in front of the church building and greeted him enthusiastically. He smiled and said, "Hi," but did not move from the spot where he stood. He glanced quickly at me, his eyes unsure. He looked down and scuffed his shoes on the pavement, his hands in his pockets.

"Let's go in," I said, looking toward the church activities building. "The meeting must be about to start."

Dennis cleared his throat. "Well, yes," he said, still staring at the ground. He glanced up briefly, smiled in embarrassment and added, "I mean, it actually starts at eight."

"But you told me seven, for an hour," I expostulated. "My mother's coming to pick me up at eight."

He blushed. "Well, I know," he stammered, "The scout meeting starts at eight. Mutual starts at seven."

"Mutual?" I asked. I had heard other students refer to Mutual, but I had no clear idea what it was, only that it was a church group some teenagers went to.

"Okay," I said. "I'll go to Mutual with you." I had grown curious about Mormonism, and I longed to go camping in the High Uintas. "Then I'll come out and ask my mother if she can come back at nine."

Dennis finally mastered his confusion. "You have to be a Mormon to go to Mutual, and you have to go to Mutual to go to the scout meeting," he said.

I almost burst out with, "Well, I'll be a Mormon then," the seduction of those mystical mountains pulled me so strongly. Instead, I nodded and said, calmly, "Oh, okay." We stood in uneasy silence for a moment. Then I added, his growing discomfort palpable, "I guess you should head in now or you'll be late for Mutual. I can wait out here for my mom."

He expelled a relieved breath and said, "Yeah, okay. See you in school." He turned and made rapidly for the front steps of the building, his splay-footed gait clopping on the concrete. He did not look back.

Zoe Ann's father came to pick me up for the prom. He waited in the car with two other ninth-grade couples while she came to the door. My parents had scraped together the money to buy me a Navy-blue suit for the dance and for graduation. A white shirt and a blue tie matching the color of my eyes completed the outfit. Zoe Ann wore a dark-blue formal that bared her shoulders and the top of her chest.

In those days, girls bought the boys boutonnieres, which they affixed to the buttonhole of the left lapel of the boy's suit coat. Boys bought the girls aromatic corsages, which they were supposed to pin to the top left side of the girl's formal. The latter always proved to be a tricky maneuver. Somehow, you were supposed to work the pin through the top of the dress without touching or stabbing the perfumed breast right beneath it. Clumsiness prevailed, with lots of fumbling and held breath. But Zoe Ann seemed completely at ease and even helped me work the pin through the fabric and fasten the gardenia corsage firmly in place. My mother hovered in the background.

The dance took place in the school gymnasium, adorned with crepe paper bunting, streamers and colorful signs of welcome strung over the door. Refreshment stands stood along the sides, and a dance combo had arranged itself on the stage. Dim lighting left the middle of the room in near darkness. Couples thronged the floor. Parents, mine among them, sat in the bleachers as guests and chaperones.

The musicians struck up lively tunes to begin with— jitterbugs and quick two-steps, with a vigorous waltz or two interspersed. Zoe Ann and I danced primarily with each other. I did not know the girls in the other two couples, and the few times we exchanged partners, conversation ran haltingly and we gladly returned to our dates. Zoe Ann evinced little interest in dancing with the other two boys after our obligatory exchanges.

We paused for refreshments when the band took a break or when the pace of the dancing called for us to cool off. The sugary Kool-Aid served to quench our thirst as Zoe Ann and I made polite, innocuous conversation. In truth, I did not know Zoe Ann much better than I knew the other girls, even though we had talked a bit about school and classes on the drive in.

After their mid-dance rest, the musicians slowed the tempo and close dancing began. Zoe Ann readily pressed herself to me and laid her head against my shoulder. My right arm circled her waist more fully and I gradually drew her right hand close between us with my left. Our steps slowed in response to the beat, our feet now close beside each other so that I could sometimes feel her thighs against mine. The smell of crushed gardenia, crumpled carnation, perfume and adolescent desire arose between our bodies.

I moved in bliss. In my innocent mind, I thought this was as good as it could get. The only fly in this otherwise sensuous ointment was the thought of my parents sitting in the stands. I steered Zoe Ann into the largest groups of other couples, hoping they would not distinguish me in the crowd. I did not worry about my father, but I feared my mother's wrath. My budding manhood frightened her and aroused her moralistic fervor. I knew this wonderfully romantic and sexual experience would meet with her powerful censure. So, while Zoe Ann and I clung to each other, barely moving, my body remained tense and my mind raced.

At this moment, Zoe Ann stepped back, slid her left hand from around my neck and said, "C'mon." She led me by the hand, threading her way expertly through the other dancers and out into the hall. I thought maybe she wanted a breath of fresher air or a rest, but instead, she drew me into a space under one of the staircases, leaned her back against the wall, tilted her head up and looked at me with liquid eyes.

Understand, I had never kissed anyone outside my family before. I knew what she wanted, and I wanted it, too, but I had no idea how to go about it. I asked uncertainly, "May I kiss you?"

She nodded, hiding whatever impatience she might have felt, and leaned forward slightly. I bent and pressed my closed lips to her mouth for a moment. Her lips were wet, warm, vibrant and open. I pulled back. I had heard about French kissing, but this took me by surprise. I had supposed that you led up to it gradually. How to proceed? I leaned down again, my lips not quite so compressed and held the kiss for longer.

But this moment jarred my romantic imagination. I had pictured a candle-lit, private room with soft furniture, not a concrete stairwell with fluorescent lighting, open to any passerby or, God forbid, a chaperone who had seen us leave. My kisses became not only inept, but unwilling.

"I think we should go back," I said, straightening up. "I don't think we're supposed to be out here." She hid whatever disappointment or irritation might have arisen in her and followed me docilely back into the gym. We danced one or two more numbers, but soon the lights came up, the musicians packed their instruments, and everyone began to stream toward the door and the waiting cars.

After Dennis had disappeared into the meeting hall, I took stock of my surroundings. I had shopped with my mother in a grocery store in Tooele. Other than that, I had never been off the school property. I decided to explore the neighborhood.

Quiet reigned. The school grounds lay empty, the building dark. Small, flimsily built houses lined the nearby streets. Military installations near the town had provided much of the employment during the war. Construction companies, under government contract and tight timelines, had hastily flung up these structures to house workers and their families. A few older, more solid buildings stood interspersed among the flimsy ones, with mature plantings around them.

I came across many half-finished houses, clearly occupied, with cars parked in front. These consisted of cinderblock foundations rising about knee-high, covered with temporary, flat plywood roofs nailed over with thick tarpaper. In each, a concrete stairway descended below that roof, with a solid wooden door at the bottom. People—whole families—lived in these basements, waiting to accumulate the wherewithal to build the above-ground story. I admired their ingenuity and determination, but I found myself sad for them. My family had suffered deprivation, but had always lived with sunlit windows and open air.

My mother arrived early to pick me up. Surprised to see me standing alone outside, exactly where she had dropped me off, she questioned me as soon as I opened the car door. My explanation startled her.

"Boy Scouts are nonsectarian," she burst out. "You don't have to belong to any one religion. That's wrong!"

I didn't argue with her, but I didn't share her indignation either. For some reason, being excluded didn't upset me much. I had had a good time on my own. I just said, "Well, I guess in Tooele you do." My calmness quieted her and we talked of other things the rest of the way home. Many years later, I discovered that the Boy Scouts did make an exception, especially in Mormon country. They allowed the church to sponsor troops specifically for members of its religion.

Dennis apologized at school the next day. We still talked and did algebra problems together. A certain constraint hung over our friendship, but we were cordial enough. I held no ill feelings. The awkwardness lay on his part. In any case, I knew that if all went as planned for my father's work, I wouldn't attend school there the next year. Much as I liked Dennis, the impossibility of a close friendship with a devout Mormon did not weigh on me.

Zoe Ann's father drove me home just as he had picked me up, with the two other couples in the car. I wondered why he did not drop them off first, since they lived in Tooele. I would have welcomed the chance to exchange a few words with him, polite boy that I was. But I did not ask, and he did not speak to any of us.

I sat directly behind him, one of four people crammed into the back seat, with Zoe Ann beside me. She took my right arm and draped it over her shoulder. She continued to hold my right hand with hers, fingering and stroking my palm and occasionally pulling it close to her breast. The aroma of crushed flowers and sweat from six young bodies permeated the air. The infrequent muttering of the other couples, who were evidently at ease with each other, rolled around unintelligibly inside the car. Zoe Ann and I did not speak. Her father maintained his silence.

Zoe Ann seemed remarkably uninhibited, as if her near-sexual cuddling with me in her father's presence were completely normal. I, on the other hand, sat nervous and apprehensive. Every time I looked up from Zoe Ann's face and body, I met her father's stern, suspicious, warning eyes boring into mine from the rearview mirror.

I half expected him to jerk the car to a stop, drag me out, beat me up and leave me by the side of the road for molesting his daughter if I allowed Zoe Ann to pull my hand against her inviting breast. Lord knows, I wanted to do that, and more. But fear overmastered my desires and Zoe Ann's obvious willingness.

When he pulled up in front of my house, all too soon and yet none too soon, I unstuck myself from Zoe Ann, extracted myself from the car, thanked my date for a wonderful evening, and thanked her father for the ride. I dared not kiss her, despite her upturned face and melting, chocolate eyes. Relief rode over me, alloyed with gentle sadness about what might have been, as I watched the taillights disappear over the rise, then turned and walked through the fresh May night into the house.

I don't remember seeing Zoe Ann again during the final week of school. I wore the same blue suit to graduation. My family drove into town under a spectacular, pastel sunset. I sat in the back seat behind my father, who kept his eyes on the road and spoke to my mother beside him. I leaned my head against the cool glass of the window and let it bump softly as the tires rolled over the uneven pavement. "Red Sails in the Sunset" was playing on the car radio. I dreamed of distant lands and romantic adventures.

8

Seeing If I Could Kill My Father

Oedipal issues ran rife in my family. I imagined killing my father. We kept guns, and I pictured loading up my father's hunting rifle, sneaking into my parents' bedroom and shooting him in his sleep. I saw my mother as grateful and happy. However, that vision always shifted, ending with my easing off the trigger, snapping the safety back on and retreating silently. I fell on the law-abiding side of my passionate ambivalence.

Only later did I dream of sleeping with my mother, although, as a young boy, I often woke from a nightmare or simple fear to crawl into my parents' bed and snuggle against her body. Something more than mere comfort held me there and, I believed, kept her holding me to her, until my father's disgruntlement expelled me.

Early in my life, I wrestled with my father. That sport, like boxing, attracted me. We tussled in good humor; I asked him to teach me. He was not a competitive wrestler himself, but he demonstrated a few holds, gently and carefully. I relied on his strength and love to prevent injury and keep us safe. We were a physically active family anyway—running, hiking, hunting, camping, engaging in sports of all kinds. Bodily contact energized me, as it did my parents. Violence played little part; eros in the sense of essential vitality impelled us. But the potential for aggression lurked.

My parents resorted to corporal punishment rarely, but explosively. My sister bore most of my mother's wrathful spankings. I remember her screams and flailing as my mother walloped her with a hairbrush. I stoically endured my father's few but severe whippings and cuffings. These incidents exacerbated my already latent feelings, especially since my mother never struck me physically and my father spared my sister. My brother—the youngest—lived under my mother's protection and my father's benign inattention.

Psychology tells us that two developmental periods stimulate Oedipal sexual issues to particular intensity. The ages from two or three to five or six encompass the first; early adolescence marks the second. Usually, the first, while more overt because the child has not yet learned to dissemble, provokes more amusement than challenge.

A memory of my son comes to mind. When Andrew was five, he, my wife Celia, and I were having breakfast one workday morning. I had dressed for the office and classroom. Andrew was sitting between Celia and me as we ate our Cheerios. A record of *Beauty and the Beast*—one of Andrew's favorites—was playing on the phonograph. The strong New York accent of the man performing the role of the beast struck me. I imitated it, comically, I thought, and probably uttered a disparaging remark sotto voce.

Miniskirts had come into fashion, and Celia was wearing a particularly skimpy one. After I had spoken, Andrew put down his spoon, reached over, placed the palm of his small, soft hand high up on her bare thigh, pressed down, turned his face up to me, fixed his serious, imperative blue eyes on mine and said, "You could go to work now, Dad!"

My father would not have brooked such insolence or understood its source. Even when I was young, my parents demanded respect and did not abide anything they considered an abrogation of that. Underlying emotions hardly counted, behavior did.

Early adolescence provoked more covert but powerful struggles for me. That period coincided with the year we lived in Bauer. One late morning on a dry, autumn weekend, when I was on the cusp of fourteen, I suggested to my father that we go out and wrestle. If any incident or discussion precipitated my proposal, I don't recall it, but I was at loose ends and filled with jumpy energy. My father nodded, and out we went, onto the dirty, sparse patch of front lawn.

We had not engaged each other in physical contest for years. Awkwardly, we grappled, I on the offensive, since I had proposed the match, he defending with a strength and deftness that surprised and challenged me. As I warmed up, I forced the issue and brought us both to the ground, I on my back and he on his knees. I had recently read about a powerful, bout-ending scissor hold. I wrapped my legs high around his waist, crossed my ankles behind him and began to squeeze.

We locked eyes. His reddened face paled, then blotched white and crimson. His rib cage compressed under my pressure. I was panting with effort, the hard earth roughing my back and nape as I strained.

He reared back slightly, lifted my torso and head off the ground and thumped them down. Not hard, but a clear warning. Dust rose around me, acrid with the scent of desiccated cottonwood leaves and twigs.

Our combat transpired in utter silence save for my panting, his increasingly shallow and stertorous breathing, and the thud of my skull and body rhythmically striking the ungiving ground. The harder I constricted, the higher he lifted me; the more sharply he dropped me, the more severely it hurt. Our battle had turned serious; we were no longer playing. I struggled to overcome him, to force him to submit; he strove to teach me an unforgettable lesson.

Endurance and fortitude marked my character, but before long I realized that I was losing. Anger and determination, touched by surprise and fear, showed in his stare. Perhaps to save some face—after all, I had initiated this battle—I pushed on for a few more seconds, but my father's shallow, desperate breathing began to frighten me. The unremitting thumping made my head ache without pause. My legs, in their vise grip, began to weaken and cramp. Dust and dead leaves puffed from the sides of my trunk as my father slammed it down.

I raised a hand to signal a stop and unhooked my ankles. My legs fell away from my father's sides and he rocked back, sweat pasting the twisted strands of his hair to his balding scalp. Our eyes, his bloodshot now, still met. Our breathing gradually eased as I lay and he knelt, leaning back on his heels. We still had not spoken, but our battle had satisfied something in both of us.

In his face, I read not only triumph but also respect, tinged with uncertainty. I had never challenged him so directly before; it confused him, as did my ability and willingness to hurt him physically. He had won, and accomplished it without destroying me, his son. Competitive man that he was, that victory gave him pleasure and would have no matter his opponent. He also respected me for my aggressiveness, my strength and my capacity to endure the pounding without whimper or complaint. He had always worried that I might not make my way in the masculine world. This episode reassured him. I had fought well and I had not cried uncle; I had simply terminated the struggle when we both knew it was time.

For my part, disappointment, relief and my own confusion rode through me. Having overestimated my strength and stamina, used as I was to encountering boys my own age, dismayed me. At the same time, my father's strength and canniness in our war reassured me. For the few years before this, I had lost connection with him. He worked long hours and had also ceded much of the emotional and moral, as well as physical, leadership of the family to my mother. As I lay on the packed earth, my pain subsiding, my father's triumph and my own defeat had put the world in its right order for the moment.

Still, my confusion remained in the settling dust. I could not grasp what had happened, *why* I had fought him with such a naked desire to hurt him, to conquer him. Only years, decades, later did I realize that I wanted to replace him but, at the same time, I feared to. I longed for clarity as to who headed the family.

I slid my eyes from his, pulled my knees up to my chest and rolled away, avoiding any contact with him. Clumsily, I stood up from all fours. My father gathered himself and stumbled to his feet. We brushed and thwacked the dust, twigs and crushed leaves from our clothes. We straightened our spines, squared our shoulders in unison and took a slow, deep breath.

We half turned toward each other, and our glance met embarrassedly, then veered away. Half-smiles came to our lips as we looked up at the hazy September sky, its pale blue slotting through the shriveled cottonwood foliage. I nodded toward the house. "Mom probably has lunch ready." He jerked his chin up in reply, turned, and we headed for the steps, him leading and me behind.

9

Blowing Up Bauer

"Here, lemme do it. Yer doing it wrong. Yuh hafta stick it in the ground," he growled, grabbing a sky rocket from the pile and waving his flashlight around my feet.

"It won't go up," I thought. The rocket itself was bound securely to the stick that he jammed into the ground. But I did not speak, I a fourteen-year-old boy and he a rough-cob miner. He demanded a match, struck it on the seat of his Levi's, put it to the fuse, and we all stood back.

The fuse tucked into the powder, the rocket took fire and flared in place for many seconds, spewing sparks at our feet. It exploded softly, in a blaze of color that made us spring back, then died. The man remained mute, the burned match between his stubby fingers.

"Ha," I thought. "I knew my first one was a dud. That's why it didn't take off." I bent down for another one and slid the stick into the pipe I had wedged between some rocks as a launcher. I scraped the match head on a stone, lit the fuse, and the rocket soared into the night sky, showering a spectacular arc of colored streamers.

The big cardboard box had arrived from California in mid-June. I had read the ad in a magazine or maybe even on the back of a matchbook: "Fireworks! Complete set, from sparklers and snakes to sky rockets and Roman candles."

They had not exaggerated. I cut open the box excitedly, but carefully, to find a vast array that exceeded my expectations. I unwrapped layers, ranging from the advertised gray, cylindrical snakes and star-shaped sparklers through pounds of firecrackers. Strings of poppers lay over explosives of various dimensions and shapes, ending in cherry bombs and three-inch salutes, those cardboard cylinders of black powder. Scores of nighttime fireworks rounded out the kit.

I gazed in awe at the assortment. I called to my brother, and we spread the fireworks out over our beds and the floor of our room, examining them all. Then, with happy anticipation, we packed them back in the box. Years of Christmases had taught us delayed gratification; we would wait until the Fourth itself.

Independence Day dawned clear and sunny. Before the rest of the family had awakened or the settlement had stirred, we carried the box to the front stoop and took out a few of the smaller devices, just to start things off. We figured the noise would invigorate the meager population of the settlement and provide a celebratory initiation of the holiday.

We began slowly, with a few strings of poppers. We tried a sparkler or two, but decided that they would serve more effectively at night, and also that we should save some of them for our sister, who might like them better. (She was not a fan of loud explosives.) The snakes, it turned out, unwound in amazing fashion and left interesting, and potentially startling, piles of ash on the front steps.

No one emerged from the house. We decided to up the ante. We pawed through the box and found some real firecrackers, which we set off on the dirt path outside the front gate. They made a louder bang and spewed grit. The smell of burned black powder hung in the cool, early air. The odor stimulated my imagination. I pictured Fort McHenry and our tattered flag still flying. World War II was less than six years behind us, and the Korean War had begun. Battle images permeated my world.

No passersby appeared. The holiday allowed people to stay abed or at least at home. We checked inside our house, but it lay silent. My sister kept to herself that year, but our parents usually woke early. We decided to see if we could rouse them.

We selected a thick, two-inch salute from the box. I had found an old, empty milk can in the garage. I figured if we put the cracker in the metal can, it would help the explosion resonate. We crept through the old briars and vines that cluttered the untended side of the house, keeping an eye out for bull snakes and black widows, until we crouched just under our parents' bedroom window. We whispered conspiratorially.

I struck a wooden match on the cinder-block foundation of the house, touched the flame to the fuse, whipped the match out, dropped the charge into the can and covered my ears. The blast outdid our hopes. It reverberated in the can and against the wall. We waited, stifling our laughter.

No voices came from the room. The shade did not go up. Squatting beneath the window, I retrieved the smoking can, now warm to the touch, and we threaded our way back through the thorns. Though we had failed to panic our parents awake, the satisfying experiment with the milk can offered new possibilities.

I suppose we ate breakfast at some point. And eventually, my father came out to observe and encourage us. My mother and sister wandered out briefly, lit a few sparklers and worms to placate our enthusiasm, then retired to the relative seclusion of the house. But we concentrated our energy on creating more varied and larger explosions.

We scoured the surroundings for empty metal containers of any kind. We stuck crackers of various sizes in and under the cans. We experimented with which cracker it took to blow a can up into the limbs of the cottonwood or out into the street. We practiced lighting two or three fuses simultaneously to create an even more gratifying *kaboom!*

When these exercises began to pall, we ranged farther afield. In the dry ditch across the road, we buried the biggest salutes under clods of packed clay and pretended the eruptions were land mines or mortar shells. We ignited multiple strings of smaller crackers to simulate machine-gun fire and dove for cover in our simulated combat.

The path and ditch began to resemble miniature battlefields, with torn-up earth, constant blasts in our ears and the odor of burned black powder hanging in the summer air. Of course, I had no conception of actual armed battles. I associated our vigorous activity and playacting with valorous, bloodless exploits. I did not envision the carnage that actual warfare entails.

After a break for lunch, we went at it again. Naval images floated into my mind. I wondered if the stiff, cherry-bomb fuses would stay lit under water. We amassed a pile of them and trotted down to the guppy pond. I set a match to one and tossed it out into the murky water. It sank with a fizzle. We waited eagerly. Just as the ripples had faded and I was turning away in disappointment, we heard a soft thud. The ground shook slightly and, as we watched, a large bubble of white smoke broke the surface and burst softly.

Guppies swarmed to the surface and writhed in all directions. One or two of their compatriots rose belly up. We had dropped a successful depth charge. Pretending we had spotted enemy submarines, we sidled around the bank, pushing our way through willows and bombarding our imagined foe.

I had speculated on whether some bigger fish, like carp or bass, probably malformed and hostile, lurked in the foul depths. If so, I hoped the explosions would flush them to the surface, but none appeared. I came to suppose that the thousands of guppies had the water, such as it was, to themselves.

As we had been celebrating, neighbors and other denizens had gradually emerged. They nodded or chatted in approval. The settlement held only about forty inhabitants. No one else had fireworks. A couple of other, younger boys wandered by and stopped to stare. After carefully instructing them, we let them set off, under our watchful supervision, some of the smaller crackers and the last of the snakes.

Through these interactions, word spread that we had an ample store of nighttime munitions. With our parents' approval, we invited everyone to an amateur fireworks display, starting at dusk. We identified the location as the rocky outcropping above the mine, where the earth lay barren and little chance of an accidental conflagration existed.

After taking a break to eat supper and plan, we loaded all the evening fireworks into the box. Being sticklers for tradition, we intended to set off explosives only on the Fourth, so we lit the last of the crackers on the dirt track, picked up our load, and the whole family set off, trailed by three-quarters of the population of Bauer and one or two visitors.

Several people carried flashlights. I had grown up trained to see in the night outdoors. We owned flashlights, but I rarely used one. The randomly darting beams disconcerted me as we made our way over and around the sharp boulders—there was no trail—until we arrived at the flat patch on top of the outcrop.

We handed around sparklers to create a festive atmosphere. Neither my brother nor I had any experience with rocketry, and the shipment contained no instructions. We had thought about it, however, and strategized. The first rocket I had lit had failed to launch and it was at this point that the dictatorial miner tried to take over. As he stood there fingering the charred matchstick, I fired the first successful shot of the evening, to his disgruntlement and everyone else's pleasure. The girls screamed, oohed and aahed and the boys and men gazed in appreciation.

Roman candles showed themselves to be trickier, because, against all warnings, you had to hold those in your hand for best effect. After a try or two, I found the rhythm and learned to pump my arm upward just as the next ball of brilliant fire emerged. The bright spheres rose high and beautiful against the dark sky.

The box also included several devices called atomic wings. They proved unpredictable and wildly arousing. Shaped like a two-bladed, colored airplane propeller, they lay passively on the ground until ignited, at which point they rose swiftly and erratically. You had no idea where they would head. Sometimes onlookers had to duck and dodge as the wings darted hither and yon until they attained altitude. Then they emitted wondrous bursts of streamers, sparks and stardust.

I should note that we did all of this with no protective equipment whatsoever. We wore no gloves or glasses. We shrugged off the occasional match or powder burn. In those days, cars did not carry seat belts; bikers, skiers and baseball players did not don helmets; hockey goalies did not wear masks. Stuntmen in street clothes still walked on the wings of flying biplanes. For us children, safety simply meant being careful and shrugging off injury if you could.

I noticed, as our display was nearing its climax, that a couple of teenage girls, one of them older than I and a stranger, were drawing closer to me. In my innocence, I knew nothing about the exciting effects of spiraling colors against the night sky or the attractiveness of martial prowess. As the Roman candles ejaculated their comely spheres, however, and the spewing of the rockets grew wider and more vivid, the girls' magnetic pull toward me increased. As the last bomb exploded and the sparks drifted away into the slag heap, the more mature of the girls took my hand and whispered, "Thank you. That was just wonderful! So exciting!"

The crowd dispersed as my brother and I cleaned up the empty casings and other detritus. People expressed their appreciation on their way past, talking softly among themselves. As we made our stumbling way over the rocks and boulders, now in the full dark, the girl hung close. She took my hand again. In the starlight, she looked luminous and very pretty. "Help me," she pleaded softly. "I'm afraid I might trip."

"Certainly," I responded as I began to guide her, half the young gentleman that my mother had trained me to be, and half the yearning, adolescent boy that I had become.

We made our way through the pile of rubble, her hand warm in mine, I stumbling as much as she. Her breath quickened with each hesitant step; I tried to contain mine. She thanked me repeatedly until we reached open ground and the road.

My parents and hers stood waiting. I awkwardly unstuck my sweaty palm from hers as she joined her family, and I mine. "See you around," she said, as she took her mother's arm and they headed off.

My father smiled at my brother and me. "That was a good show, boys!"

"Did you get everything?" my mother asked. My brother held out the box and I said, "Yes, I think so."

We strolled home together. For once, I felt safe in the fold of my family and relieved to be there. My brother and I discarded the remains. We had some warm milk and chocolate cookies together before we called it a day. Roman candles and dark-eyed girls lit my way to bed.

10

Bull Snakes by the Furnace

I tug the stiff, asbestos mitts onto my chilled hands as I look warily around the cobwebbed basement. High in the cinder-block wall, cold air blows through the broken window. Early light outlines the jagged edges in blue. The remaining shards jut, translucent. I bend and twist open the furnace door, the coiled handle still warm. I lift the heavy steel tongs and poke them in to seize a piece of the black clinker rimming the still-glowing fire.

That was my job in Bauer—to tend to the furnace, our sole source of heat. I had assigned myself the task. I wanted to help the family that difficult year, and I prided myself on my capability to do a man's job. Years earlier, I had observed and even tried my boyhood hand in the blacksmith shop at the mine where my father worked. I now imagined the smith's pride in his erstwhile apprentice.

To get to my work, I had to make my way down a rickety flight of broken stairs without a handrail. At the top, I braced myself against the walls and then one of the splintery joists as I ducked under it. On the last four steps, I balanced with arms outstretched, like a tightrope walker, as the aging wood sagged and creaked under me.

The first time I descended, as fall was setting in and the nights were growing chill, I heard a rustling and loud hiss as I stepped out onto the cellar floor. A giant bull snake unwound itself from beside the furnace and jabbed its open mouth toward me. I stumbled back, terrified, searching for some weapon to defend myself. I knew little about snakes. In northern Idaho, I had encountered only small, harmless garter snakes and little, brown water snakes. I had heard about poisonous reptiles in the desert, though, and instinctively, if mistakenly, assumed I was facing one.

At my sudden reaction, however, it thrust its weaving, upraised head at me once more, emitted a final, loud hiss, swerved and boiled over the coal scuttle, up the wall and out the bottom of the window frame where no glass remained. With a softer rustle and no hiss, a shorter, thinner companion slithered from behind a cracked pallet and swiftly followed, with a goodbye flick of its tail tip.

I warily cased the rest of the basement for more serpents. I found none, but I couldn't be sure in the semi-darkness. Frequently glancing over my shoulders and up at the window, I turned my attention to building a wood fire in the dormant furnace, to heat the metal and prepare a hot bed to start the fuel. In rural areas such as Bauer, many people, including my family, still heated their houses with plentiful, cheap, soft coal. Few concerned themselves with the air pollution it caused. "It blows away," men would say. "In five minutes, you can't even see it."

I laid shavings and kindling inside, with spaces for air to circulate. I struck a match on the sooty door and stretched in to hold the flame under the loose stack until the first pieces caught. I loved building fires. I had learned the skill from my father on family camping trips. I took pride in my craft. My parents trusted me to do it well and safely, without supervision.

I fed in larger sticks as the fire grew. Hot air pulled upward through the open flue until the flames began to heat the iron walls. The sides of the furnace popped and clanged as they expanded, radiating warmth into the room.

As the conflagration died down, I reached for the narrow shovel and deposited several lumps of coal in the center of the bed. At first, I feared I had put the fire out as the flames caved around the black pile. But soon the outer facets of the coal began to glow, until the whole heap turned a pulsing orange-red. Pleased, I added a few more chunks for good measure. I returned the shovel to the hod and clamped the furnace door tight.

Checking once more for reptiles—I feared the noise might have roused others from the dark corners and they would come slithering toward the heat—I made my precarious way up the stairs into the kitchen. My family had gathered by then, and my mother was preparing a pot of hot cereal. She smiled at me as I made my way to the bathroom to wash up and dress for school. We all ate breakfast together and

set off into our days, I, with my brother and sister, on the
school bus to Tooele.

In those cold months, the boys' and girls' gyms opened
for noon hour as well as PE. Tired of wandering the halls
after lunch, I sometimes dropped in there in hopes of finding comradeship in team athletics. But the close friendship
of boys who had grown up together excluded me. Ready-
made basketball and volleyball teams competed. They side-
lined me.

The day I first heated the furnace, another outcast at
school, Dino Karabatsos, approached me and struck up a
conversation. His swarthy skin glistened and his muscles
bulged under his T-shirt. After we had exchanged a few
words, he asked if I would spar with him. No one else, he
said, wanted to join him. He confided proudly that he was
already a regionally ranked amateur middleweight and
needed to train.

My early boyhood fantasies of becoming a boxer, as I
listened to Joe Louis's bouts on the radio, re-arose briefly.
At the same time, I quickly recalled the two instances in
my young life when I had already been knocked out. When
I was ten, the metal bar of a swiftly spinning merry-go-
round caught me on the left side of the head. I came to,
staring up at the limbs of a cherry tree some fifteen feet
away. When I was thirteen, just a year before we moved to
Bauer, I had driven in for a layup in a junior high basketball
practice and smashed my temple against an unpadded steel
stanchion supporting the balcony at the end of the court.
I awoke to the ministrations of the coach, holding a vial of

ammonia to my nose, then rubbing my cheekbones and asking anxiously, "Are you all right, Steve?"

Looking at Dino's thick neck and muscular build, and not wanting to repeat my former experiences, I demurred. But he persisted until I began to reconsider. Finally, he assured me that he would practice defense only, and not strike me. I acceded.

He led me to a small room off the main gymnasium. Boxing gear, wrestling mats and exercise equipment crowded the space. The air hung close with the odor of old leather and sweat. Dino showed me around briefly, then picked two pairs of gloves off a railing where they were dangling to air out. He helped me tie on mine—two large, red cushions—and donned his. We began to spar.

Dino kept his word. He held his hands in front of his face, bobbing a bit, and did not try to punch me. I tentatively began to jab at him, but could not penetrate his southpaw defense. My blows landed harmlessly on his gloves. He encouraged me not to be timid, and even coached me a little on effective stance, hand position and timing.

Under his tutelage, I grew more aggressive. I began to imagine his stolid, dark face, as he ducked and blocked, as the weaving head of a hissing bull snake. I strove to whack that head once and for all. I punched more strongly. The few times I did manage to land a blow, Dino praised me, although I could tell it did not rock him. He hoped I would develop into an equal opponent against whom he could test his skill.

But my slender arms were built for basketball and baseball. I tired more quickly than he did and asked to rest more and more frequently. He remained patient and tried to hearten me, but even the vision of blasting the bull snake ceased to embolden my exhausted body. In addition, the dark isolation of the stuffy room, jumbled with tired equipment and gear, soon told on my spirits. After two or three such bouts, I apologetically begged off, and he eventually found another, more satisfying, opponent.

All the same, I often thought of Dino, of our sparring, and of my own boyhood Joe Louis fantasies, as I persevered in my morning and evening ritual in the furnace room. I descended the unreliable stairs in trepidation, on the *qui vive* for lurking serpents. As I donned the stiff mitts, I recalled the fat boxing gloves Dino had provided me. Unlatching the furnace door and poking in the long, heavy tongs, I lifted out the hard clinkers surrounding the still-glowing coals, heard the sudden hiss as I dunked them in the standing bucket of water, then dropped them in the hundred-gallon scrap barrel. When I had removed all the waste, I piled in enough fuel to last for the next half day, arranging the lumps carefully to allow ventilation between them.

All of this ceremony I performed with tingling in my spine, buttocks and scrotum. I imagined snakes behind and around me. Certainly, they would prefer the warmth of the furnace environs, with its local population of mice, to the icy outdoors. I did not yet know enough about herpetology to understand that reptiles, too, sought and found adequate shelter for themselves outdoors in freezing weather. I constantly glanced at the broken window where snow sometimes sifted in. I pictured the serpents writing back through the frame to drive me out and renew their residence.

None of that ever took place, and, with the gentle breath of spring in the air, I closed up the furnace for the last time and let the fire die. My parents appreciated my work. My father especially honored my competence and budding manhood. He had begun to respect me as a prospective adult companion as well as a son. My mother responded with smiles and a warmth she did not otherwise show, although she may have believed such responsibilities rightfully fell to my father. My puberty and growing masculinity both pleased and frightened her.

As for myself, I was slowly finding my way, balancing aggression and fear against tenderness and love, independence against reliance, separation against connection, all in a whirl of emotions and thoughts I kept mostly to myself. Bull snakes and fists assailed my dreams; romance and adventure soothed them.

11

Armed Hikes and Baseball

I loved the heft of the old Remington pump-action .22. My father's .30-30 hung too heavy in my hand, the recoil plowed painfully into my immature shoulder, and the explosion of the shell stunned me. But the .22 came up easily, I could hold the open sight steady, and the pop of the cartridges sounded gently in my ear.

My father had brought the smaller gun west with him in the 1930s. We often took it on hikes and always on camping trips. From an early age, my brother, sister and I learned to shoot. My parents instilled in us the lessons of careful firearm handling: Never aim a loaded weapon at something you don't intend to shoot. Keep the muzzle pointed at the ground or sky until you are ready to fire. Always stand behind the shooter. Check and check again as you empty the chamber. Clean the bore thoroughly with Hoppe's No. 9 after each use, and wipe the barrel and wooden stock down with oil. Store guns and ammunition separately.

Armed Hikes and Baseball

A boyhood hunting accident had given my father ample reason for precaution. When he was fourteen, during World War I, a friend and he had been out hunting rabbits. Carrying loaded double-barrel shotguns, they walked along a dirt roadside, my father in the lead. As my father searched for game in the grassy ditch, his friend fell into a military reverie. He pretended that he had captured a German prisoner and lowered his 20-gauge at my father's torso, safety off, with his twitchy index finger at the ready.

A rabbit sprang from cover and sprinted across the road, my father swung around and raised his gun, the friend jerked on his trigger and blasted my father in the lower left abdomen. The force knocked him to the ground. His companion panicked, threw his gun into the bushes and dashed helter-skelter, yelling. As my father attempted to rise, his intestines began to fall out. He tried to contain them with his hands as he lay back down. His friend proving useless, my father waited in shock and growing agony until, eventually, a gray-bearded farmer with a horse-drawn cart came by. The farmer shook his head as he looked at the wound and said, "I don't think you'll make it, but I'll take you into town."

With my father holding his insides together, the farmer loaded him in and jolted him over dirt roads to the town hospital. The doctor, a family friend, inspected the hole in my father's belly and merely asked calmly, "Do you want to live, Dick?" When my father nodded, he said, "Well, then, I'll do my part; you do yours."

They took out all the intestine they couldn't repair, removed as much buckshot as they could find, and sewed him back up. The next couple of years, he had to take it easy and not play rough sports, but he recovered despite the lack of antibiotics and the basic level of surgery available at the tiny hospital. When he stood naked in our bathroom, I could still see the scars and deep pockmarks. When he sat on the toilet, he had to raise his feet on a footstool. He chewed his food long and thoroughly before he swallowed it. Still, he was a vigorous, active man who did not give up hunting.

My father's tale struck my mind vividly, so he easily ingrained his cautions in me until they became second nature. Other people I saw dealt with their firearms more cavalierly, but his advice and example reassured me. From early boyhood, handling and caring for the .22 grew to be one of my genuine pleasures.

A few years before we moved to Bauer, my father had taken my brother and me out deer hunting one snowy December day. Large flakes fell softly. My father let me carry the .22 and take the lead, while he trailed with his high-powered rifle, and my brother walked between us. We came across some fresh deer tracks. As I stepped carefully along the hoofprints, I pictured where I would have to aim to bring a deer down with my light weapon. I followed the trail accurately, but in my inexperience, I kept my eyes on the ground, rather than pausing every few steps to look ahead, as I later learned to do.

Suddenly, the tracks veered left, out of the trees, across a small clearing and into a thicket on the far side. The marks were so fresh that bits of snow were still falling from the edges of the holes into the depressions. I thought I glimpsed the deer's rump disappearing into the evergreens, but darkness had drawn in and I suddenly doubted myself.

I asked my father to take the lead. He responded kindly, his baritone low. "No, it's past sunset now; we couldn't shoot, anyway. But you did a good job of tracking. Maybe next time we'll have more luck."

I learned a lesson about game hunting that gloomy afternoon. My father's kindness touched me, even though I felt embarrassed. Most of all, though, I remember the intimate feel of the rifle in my hand. Even in my disappointment, my affection for it warmed my cold fingers.

In Bauer, my brother and I discovered that the settlement had evidently once enjoyed a more prosperous era. On the outskirts, just off the entry road, a now-derelict baseball field showed signs of once having been a center of local activity. The large backstop remained intact, its wire mesh rusting. Small bleachers sagged on either side of the now-invisible base paths. Any indication of turf had completely disappeared, replaced by sand, blowing grit, rolling tumbleweed and anthills. Horned toads and lizards scurried. The mound had worn down flat. My brother and I uncovered the old pitcher's rubber and home plate, bent and cracked. With effort, I could imagine green grass, gloves, balls, bats, and people calling from the stands.

That desolate area did prove useful for one thing: my mother taught my sister and me the rudiments of driving a stick shift there, away from any traffic. My bucking, stalling attempts to coordinate the clutch and gas pedal left gouges in the loose earth until I finally mastered the skill, to my passengers' relief. But when my brother and I tried pitching, batting and playing one-o'-cat, the wind and bleakness drove any enjoyment out of me. My brother always wanted to continue for hours, but I soon refused to join him. That decrepit place marked Bauer's pending demise; it induced despair in me.

All the same, at that time, baseball still glowed in its preeminence as the national sport. Many small towns continued to field teams. Pickup contests popped up in every vacant space. Boys dreamed of the majors. Amateur and semipro leagues, large and small, provided summer recreation and entertainment.

My brother and I had grown up watching, following, practicing and playing baseball. My mother's Brooklyn upbringing and fond memories of watching games at Ebbets Field led me to become an avid Dodgers fan. I listened to their games on the radio and delighted in their victories. I sorrowed with them in defeat.

In Idaho, my brother and I had participated in a summer youth program and gone to evening men's games. Here in Utah, fewer opportunities presented themselves. While Tooele High had a school team in the spring, the town itself offered no summer programs for younger boys. Bauer's abandoned field lay unplayable. But Pioche Mines Company sponsored a team, composed of men and older adolescents, to compete against other organization-backed squads in the area. They practiced and hosted home games at the Tooele High School field. Eager to play, my brother and I, despite our youth, approached the coach of the Bauer team to ask if he would take us on.

He hesitated. His taut potbelly strained at his stained shirtfront as he considered. His belt disappeared low on his pelvis. His black eyes, made narrow by pockets of fat, surveyed us doubtfully, but not unkindly. "Well," he said, "You could join, I guess. I'd be glad to give you a chance. But I can't guarantee that you'd ever get in a game. It's a men's team, you know. A few high school boys, if they're good enough, and men." He paused, assessing us, then added, "And you'll have to supply all your own equipment, cleats and gloves and caps. And no uniforms."

We agreed. We both had mitts and caps. We had no cleats, but I figured we could get by with our tennis shoes. I fostered hopes that, at the least, I could take batting practice, scoop up a few grounders and shag some fly balls before the actual game began. I had not yet forsaken my early boyhood dream of pitching for the Dodgers, but realized that pitching to real hitters lay a few years ahead.

None of my hopes came to pass. The men and high school boys ignored us. During practice, the coach let us roam the outfield, but the man with the fungo bat always directed the fly balls toward the older players. The others relegated me to retrieving stray balls they had missed. Before games, warm-up for me consisted of playing catch with my brother until play started. Then I sat in the dugout with him, the coach and one or two other outsiders. The coach did not take us on road trips; we only attended home games at the high school field in Tooele.

Eventually, the coach commanded one of the other benchwarmers to play pregame catch or pepper with me. But I soon tired of sitting on the hard, sticky bench, then standing outside to make way for the regulars when they came off the field and we were at bat. During our team's time on defense, the coach continued to assure us, "I'll put you in soon, boys. Just gimme a little more time to get this group in gear. But you'll get in."

At first, I believed him. But as I huddled in the dank dugout game after game, while the summer sun shone on the rest of the world, his promises rang hollow. His wheezing breath, his bulbous, pock-marked, red nose and the way he spat tobacco juice onto the wooden floor repelled me. I longed to get away from him, the dark confines and the foul odors. My spirit drew me outside, onto the land, however desolate it might appear.

So, I quit the team, to the extent that I had ever belonged to it. I didn't tell the coach; I simply informed my brother, who continued without hesitation, and stopped going. I traded in my glove and ball cap for my knapsack and the brimmed hat my father had handed down to me.

I prized the separation I had created. Since my early boyhood, my parents lumped me and my brother together as "the boys," separate from my sister, whose character and personality actually suited mine better. In truth, that year in Bauer, my brother and I did grow closer. No other boys our age lived in the settlement, and I often welcomed his company. But our interests were already diverging and I often longed to be on my own.

Armed Hikes and Baseball

The preceding October, I had turned fourteen, the age at which my parents allowed me to take a real weapon out on my own. Afternoons, when the baseball team was practicing or playing, I scared up some lunch or a snack, ladled my canteen full of drinking water from the fifty-gallon can in the kitchen, loaded the .22 and stuck an extra box of shells in my knapsack. I picked up the rifle and set out on my solitary, armed explorations of the harsh, open countryside.

My mother had stipulated a sole prohibition: she forbade me to cross the highway some distance behind the house. Other than that, I was free to roam wherever I listed, as long as I was home by suppertime. I wandered.

Carrying a weapon created a specific alertness in me. I attuned more intently to my surroundings. I wasn't hunting. Birds sang from the sagebrush. Meadowlarks trilled. An occasional jackrabbit zigzagged away. Rodents darted and dove. Once, a coyote trotted in the distance. I had heard boys talk about shooting such "pests" for fun, but I experienced no desire to kill them. I did not view them as pests, just part of the landscape.

I kept a lookout, and ear out, for rattlesnakes, but I never saw or heard one. Small garter snakes wove their way into the brush at my footfalls. I stopped to admire their litheness, and sometimes spoke to them quietly. In fact, I often greeted the birds, the animals and the sage as I rambled. Other times, I just observed.

A railroad track ran along the top of the hillside. At night, I had heard the click and rumble of the steel wheels, and the far, haunting cry of the steam whistle at the crossing.

That August, I climbed through thigh-high thickets of brush onto the line and paced the unevenly spaced ties. I practiced walking along one of the rails. The odor of tar, oil and creosote rose in the hot summer air. I pictured the men who had built this bed—the steel drivers with their double jacks and the gandy dancers walking their shovel handles. I imagined their strength and endurance. I wondered if I could have matched them.

Often, I ended up dropping down into the barren land beyond the mine and plant. I carried a few homemade paper targets and set them against low scrub on the hillside. I shot at the bullseye and checked my accuracy. If I found a discarded can, I fired at it from various distances and watched it hop. I had a good eye and a sure hand. I always retrieved the paper and cans. We had been raised to leave no trash. I picked up as many of the empty cartridges as I could spot and slipped them into the front pocket of my khakis.

After target practice, I would stride out into the windswept wastes. Gravel and grit crunched under my shoes. Lizards scampered and froze. The vastness intimidated me. No matter how far or fast I walked, the tan and gray mountains in the distance grew no closer. I turned and made for the relative comfort of the crackling sage and bitterbrush on the uneven earth above the mine and houses.

After my last such lone and exhilarating excursion, I once again opened the steel-mesh back gate, waded through the bristly yard and stopped at the concrete stoop to unload my rifle. As I tipped the unused bullets into my hand, voices came through the open kitchen window. My brother was excitedly talking about the last game of the season. The coach had finally put him in. He had played first base in the later innings and had come up to bat twice.

When I pushed open the door, my parents greeted me and immediately asked if I had heard my brother's good news. When I shook my head, his treble voice recounted the tale of his success, with my family's warm accolades interspersed. They especially praised him for his dedication and perseverance.

As all eyes shifted away from me, I silently edged my way around the kitchen table and walked to the back storage room. I laid out the cleaning equipment on one box and sat on another. I tore off a small piece of cotton rag and worked it through the slit in the tip of the ramrod. The luscious smell of banana oil and metal solvent rose from the open bottle of Hoppe's No. 9 as I dipped the swab. Forcing the tip into the muzzle, I slid the ramrod up and down, feeling the snugness of the bore and the release as the rag popped free in the chamber. I repeated this operation devotedly until the cloth came out clean, after which I made a final run with a dry swatch.

This process absorbed my senses entirely. The smell of cleaning fluid, the coolness of the barrel and stock to my touch, the rattle of the pushing ramrod and the sight of gray-blue metal and deep-brown wood engrossed me. I smiled peacefully as I stowed the cleaning gear, stored the rifle and discarded the used scraps of material.

I did not rejoin the assembled family until supper. I picked up a novel I had been reading, sat down at my desk, gazed for a moment out the window at the waving cotton-woods, then turned my eyes to the page and drifted into a distant world.

12

Sporty

His agonized barking began at bedtime. At the first yelps, I padded out in bare feet and pajamas to the chicken-wire enclosure behind the garage, where he lay. Stars sparkled in the black sky, and chill autumn air washed around me as I felt my way. He quieted briefly as I approached, then howled anew. Sharp sticks and brittle weeds jabbed my skin through the thin cotton as I lay down beside his swollen body.

He did not recognize me. I called his name and put my arms around him, as I had done so often when we were both younger. But now he could not let me calm him; his travail was too great. He flailed, his once-sturdy legs losing strength, his uncut toenails dagging my chest.

My mother's voice sounded kindly but firmly behind me. "Steve, come in the house. It's time for bed."

"But mom, he needs me. He needs help. We have to do something. He's hurting. Can't we give him something?"

"I'm working for him, Steve. That's the best we can do. Now you get up and come in. You need your sleep. You have school tomorrow."

I got to my hands and knees, the smell of Sporty's dusty fur strong in my nostrils. My mother shone her flashlight on him briefly as I stood. His chest heaved and his glazed eyes, once so bright and happy, wandered.

"Now you go in to bed," she said. I obeyed, tears trickling down my cheeks.

Sporty had lived with us since before I could remember. He was well over twelve now, and I had just turned fourteen. A purebred English springer spaniel in the old style, with a stocky, liver-and-white body and bold, playful spirit, he had accompanied and blessed my boyhood.

My parents had not had him neutered, nor did he ever wear a collar or tag. Ungroomed, unkempt, eager and energetic, he moved through his world with power, enterprise and joy. Half-wild, unbreakably attached to our family, he complicated and enhanced our lives.

He was a lapidary dog. On cold, winter hikes, he dove off snowbanks into fast-flowing creeks. Head and body underwater in a deep pool, like a giant, furred water ouzel, he extracted a smooth river rock with his jaws and surfaced, snorting. Up onto the shore he bounded, dropped the rock in the soft snow, where it instantly disappeared, and shook himself full body, spraying me with frigid droplets. Then, baffled at the loss of his treasure, he looked down, sniffed and dug at the hole. Often, the snow lay too deep, so he gave up and dove back into the icy stream for another.

Sporty

Snow clumped on his wattles and between his pads. He lay down in the middle of the trail to chew it off, impeding our progress.

On summer camping trips, he devised a game. My mother would give him an empty pork-and-beans can. After licking it clean, he placed it carefully on the ground on one side of a fallen log near the campsite. He then proceeded briskly to the other side of the log, crouched and began gnawing at the wood and tearing furiously at the turf, trying to break through to his quarry. From time to time, he rose, trotted around the log to make sure the can remained in place, then returned to his efforts. He maintained this entertainment for hours, the stub of his tail wagging briskly the while.

Sport was a dirty dog. We never groomed him; his only baths consisted of swims in mountain lakes and rivers and dashes through the sprinkler. No one took him to the vet, and his teeth chipped and yellowed with age. Twisting his body in the gravel, he chewed off hunks of matted hair and foraged between his toes.

I loved the way he smelled, of the earth. I loved how he snuggled and played with me on the lawn, his paws and rough fur against my young hands, his breath on my face as we lay nose to nose. He may have felt the greatest attachment to my mother, who fed him. But no one else in the family shared close physical affection with him the way I did. I loved him.

I, alone, ventured into his doghouse to clean it. Built into the side of the storeroom, his dark lair required me to squeeze in on all fours and operate by feel. A baker's dozen burlap bags served as his bedding. He had further equipped his den with a multitude of chewed, dry bones and an assortment of rocks of various sizes and shapes. The ripe odor of unwashed fur, dust and a scent unique to Sporty clotted my nostrils as I crawled in.

I dragged out all the gunnysacks, shook them mightily, closing my eyes against the flying grit, and hung them on the picket fence to air. Back in I crept to retrieve the stones and bones, which I dusted and arranged in rows on the porch where the warm sun could disinfect them. I swept his floor with a whisk broom and hauled out many a dust-pan load of grime, pebbles, bone chips and unidentifiable oddments.

I did not consider this a chore. It gladdened me. The intimacy of it brought me closer to him. He would lie peacefully in the yard, observing me. He bounced up now and then to sniff his possessions, then retreated to the lawn. When I had fluffed his bedding as best I could and restored his playthings to the corners of his room, he would rise, walk languidly over, enter and paw everything into place.

I envisioned asking my mother if I could sleep in his house with him. I thought I might like that better than sharing a room with my brother. I wondered if that snug enclosure would comfort me as much as it evidently did him. Several times, as I washed my hands with the garden hose after cleaning his house, I pondered what I would experience if I actually *were* Sport, what I would sense and what I would miss. Not if I were just any dog, but Sport.

He roamed some when he was young, on the track of females in heat. My parents did not hire him out to stud, although I overheard them talk about it, and he would certainly have sired handsome progeny. He did not show aggression, but, as a young dog, and in his prime, he did not avoid a fight. He defended himself effectively and with merciless zeal.

Once, my father took Sport and me for an after-supper walk when we still lived in Mullan, Idaho. As we passed Harwood's Drug Store, I noticed a passel of high school boys hanging around the porch. Kirby Stark stood among them, his large male German shepherd beside him. Kirby enjoyed threatening younger boys with his ferocious dog.

Neither my father nor Sport heeded them. As we passed and stopped at the curb to check for cars, however, I heard Kirby whispering, "Sic 'em." The dog growled low, his teeth bared and his hackles rising. The other boys tittered, giggled and muttered encouragement to Kirby.

At the menacing sound and audible voices, Sport turned. His peaceful demeanor shifted, his sturdy body tensed, and his claws scratched at the pavement for traction. At one more, louder "Sic 'em" from the emboldened Kirby, the shepherd leapt down. With a loud snarl, Sport sprang to meet him, and the battle was joined.

The combat lasted briefly. Sport caught his opponent under the chest, knocked the wind out of him and drove him toward the porch. The shepherd's hind legs snagged on the lowest step. Regaining his breath, he yelped and squealed as Sport lifted him and threw him on his back against the concrete stairs. The shepherd's paws scrabbled and flailed as Sport, snapping and snarling, rode him up and seized his throat. The shouts and gleeful hurrahs of the gang faded to uneasy mutterings as the shepherd began to wheeze and gasp. Sport burrowed in, his chomping audible as the shepherd's legs began to wave feebly.

My father had been standing calmly, hands in the back pockets of his khakis. Kirby wavered and hesitated, his hands twitching. He'd take a step toward the combatants, then retreat nervously. Finally, as the shepherd's whole body began to go inert, my father asked quietly, "Had enough?"

At Kirby's nod, my father whistled and called, but Sport paid no heed; he was in for the kill. Slowly, still afraid of Kirby and his dog, I walked up to the steps and began to stroke Sporty's back and speak to him softly. Gradually, he released his grip and backed off. The trembling shepherd rolled and staggered to his feet, blood dripping from his neck. With a parting growl, Sport shook himself thoroughly and, wagging his stump of a tail, looked up at my father and me as if to say, "Okay, that was fun. What next?"

That vital warrior had faded as he aged. His hearing and sight, once so acute, failed him. When we left Idaho, my parents kenneled him until we landed in Utah and sent for him. That long month of separation from the only family he had known since he had been six weeks old stunned him. The dog who arrived in a crate one weekday afternoon bore little resemblance to the companion I had grown up with.

I climbed down from the school bus on that warm September afternoon to find my mother sitting in a steel, lawn chair. The shaved, trimmed, cleaned spaniel beside her sat silent, like a statue in an advertisement.

"Who is that?" I asked. I wondered for the first few seconds if she had gotten a new pet for some reason.

She smiled knowingly and nodded at the animal beside her, while I stood in confusion. She knew how much I loved Sport, so, with another nod, she finally said, "That's Sporty. Don't you recognize him? He's your dog."

I dropped my books and went to my knees beside him, arms outstretched. He did not respond, either to my voice or to my caresses. After a long pause, my mother said gently, "He's been through a lot, Steve. Let's just give him some time. He'll come back to himself."

And, indeed, he did—to the aged, twelve-year-old self that he had become. His fur grew out and his enthusiasm returned. The disinfectant smell from the kennel faded away and his gamey, outdoor odor replaced it. But his compromised faculties betrayed him. He smashed into sagebrush and tumbled into gullies he could not see. He did not hear our calls and searched frantically for us when we were downwind in the fields. But his zest for adventure and love for his family filled his hearty being once again, though for the last time.

We were Christian Scientists and believed in the healing power, not so much of prayer to God as of "knowing the truth" of the perfection of all beings. When my mother said she was "working for him," she meant she was reading the Scriptures and Christian Science texts to assert that healing truth. In her mind, she stood on solid ground, not just because of her faith, but also because she credited herself with having brought him back from death once before.

Years earlier, the whole family had been taking a late-winter hike. The snow lay deep and heavy, with thick flakes falling, as we slogged along a low ridgeline. Sport, as was his wont, raced joyously back and forth, up and down, disappearing to investigate a beguiling scent, then returning boisterously to jump on us and slow our already halting progress.

Suddenly, he stopped, collapsed, rolled limply down the steep hillside and fell out of sight into a tree well. My mother called urgently to my father, who was breaking trail. When my father turned, she pointed. They exchanged glances, my father shucked his pack basket, strode and slid quickly down until he, too, disappeared from view. The wet cold seeping in, we waited.

Shortly, my father emerged from the trees, plowed his way, slipping and catching himself, directly up the slope to my mother. They spoke briefly, their voices so low I could not make out their words.

"Let's go, children," my mother ordered as my father shouldered his pack and postholed on.

"But what about Sporty?" I asked. "Where is he? Is he alright?"

"He'll catch up," my mother said firmly. "Now let's get moving. It's getting late."

I obeyed, although, as I trod, I pictured myself waiting in the falling dusk till he reappeared, racing up the hill, panting and joyful. Or even, if need be, descending by myself, hefting his body in my arms and carrying him home.

That evening, we ate supper in somber silence, even though my mother had prepared one of our favorite after-hike meals—chili con carne on rice, with bread and butter. After we had cleaned up, she made a pot of beef stew, ladled some into a stainless-steel bowl and put it on the back porch by Sport's water bowl and doghouse.

I slept restlessly and woke apprehensive, only to find my mother in the kitchen, Christian Science books on the table, smiling broadly. "Go check the back porch, Steve," she said. I did, to find Sporty stepping out of his house, doing downward dog with his tail awag, the stew bowl licked clean.

As I later discovered, my father had reported to my mother that he had found Sport unresponsive in the tree well, with no sign of breathing or pulse. My mother had worked for him through the night, using all of her ardent, Christian Science skill. Sport had returned in the wee hours, exhausted and hungry, but apparently fully healed, a canine Lazarus.

Years later, as I trudged to bed that autumn night in Bauer, my mother settled herself at the kitchen table, her books spread out before her, to work for Sporty through the night, if need be.

His barking and howling woke me often. I resisted my longing to go be with him. Both my mother's command and the fact that I had a big test in school the next day bore down on me. Sometime in the night, the barking stopped and I fell uneasily asleep for a couple of hours, hoping that my mother's practice had again proven effective. Before first light, I twisted out of bed in the gray silence and padded quietly into the kitchen, headed for the back door. My mother sat, her books now closed neatly on the table. Her shoulders slumped and her hands lay folded in her lap.

Hoping desperately, I said, "He stopped barking in the night. Maybe he's better."

"You think so?" she responded sardonically, her blue eyes bloodshot as she stared at me bitterly.

Stung, I mumbled, "I'll go check," pointless as her tone told me it would be.

Heedless of the thorns and stones, I made my barefoot way to the pen. Sport's body lay close to the garage wall, the ground around him torn where his claws had dug in. I called his name. I looked down at him, watching vainly for his chest to rise and fall. I squatted beside him and placed my hand on his still, soft, warm body. Holding that touch, I let the tears come for some time before I straightened.

The day had dawned beautiful—frosty and clear. Birds sang in the Russian olives and cottonwoods. Small rodents rushed about their business. A raven cawed as he passed. A goose honked down by the guppy pond and a soft breeze rustled the foliage. I turned back to the house and found my mother in the same position.

"So he's dead," I said.

"Oh, is he?" she snapped, but now I saw tears beading the corners of her eyes. Later in life, I came to understand that my mother believed she had failed, that Sport's death was her fault. Christian Science, in its most adamant form, leaves little room for error. The truth of perfection and healing is there for us to grasp; illness or death represents less than adequate faith on our part.

We buried him when I got home from school—my mother, brother and I. I took charge. Getting the spade out of the garage, I led my brother partway up the hill behind the house. We quickly dug a grave in the soft earth. I climbed in and squared it to about three-by-four feet, and at least three feet deep. Hoisting myself out, I drove the spade into the loose pile beside the hole and we started back to where my mother waited beside the carcass.

We tried lifting him, but rigor mortis had set in. The soft, warm body of that morning had turned cold and rigid. His stiff legs stuck out so that we could not readily carry him, and I did not want to subject him to the indignity of being dragged. He had been a noble dog. At my suggestion, my mother brought out one of the canvas tarps that we used as ground cloths when we camped. My brother and I awkwardly raised the body, and my mother tugged the tarp under him. I seized the two front corners, my mother and brother grasped the others, we raised our surprisingly heavy load and set off.

We formed a strange funeral procession, with a canvas tarp for a coffin and two teenage boys plus a forty-seven-year-old woman as pallbearers. The hot afternoon sun glared. We struggled to keep our footing on the loose, uneven ground and panted as we worked our way up the slope. We laid our burden down beside the pile of loose dirt.

Our service consisted of short blessings and appreciations from my mother and me, and even shorter ones from my brother. I did not want to linger; for the moment, I was burying my grief along with his body. We picked up the tarp again and lowered him into the grave. He rolled halfway off the canvas as we let go. Each of us sprinkled in a handful of dirt. The particles trickled off his hide. My mother and I said goodbye to him. My brother and I filled in and mounded the grave.

I had nailed together two scraps of one-by-fours to form a crude wooden cross, with a handwritten inscription on the horizontal board. I drove the bottom of the vertical section into the head of the grave mound with the back of the spade. We stood together for a moment, staring at the upturned soil. I hoped Sporty—that free-spirited being of air and water—would forgive me for interring him. I prayed that his essence was flying high and happy in another world. Then I wiped my hands on the legs of my khakis, slung the spade over my shoulder, nodded at the other two, and we headed down.

The End

Epilogue

The Book of Bauer presents a snapshot of one year in the life of a fourteen-year-old boy and his family. From time to time, the reader may wonder about the boy's background, his past and future—where did his family come from, where did they go, and why do they interact as they do? This epilogue provides a narrative frame of reference that may answer some of those questions. Much more extensive material about the arc of that life and the fate of the family may be found in my two previous books, identified at the end of this epilogue.

My father and mother met in Schenectady, New York, in 1934. They lived across the street from each other. My thirty-year-old mother, Brooklyn born and bred and the youngest of five siblings, was caring for her terminally ill mother. My thirty-one-year-old father, raised as an only child in the hamlet of Stillwater, New York on the western bank of the upper Hudson River, was designing electric locomotives for the New York Central Railroad. The Great Depression was in full force. Their lives satisfied neither of them.

Within months of their meeting, my father lost his job, my grandmother died, my parents fell in love and, like many restless people before them, they headed west. In an old Model T Ford, they camped across the country, my mother already pregnant with my sister. They finally stopped in Reno, Nevada.

Sociable and enterprising, they quickly became friends with a professor of geology at the University of Nevada, and his wife. Through that connection, my father landed a job with a mining company in the tiny town of Austin, Nevada, in the middle of the state, on Highway 50, reputedly the loneliest highway in the country. But they thrived. They found an adobe house with a fireplace fashioned out of the local ore, made new friends and, when my father wasn't working, staked some claims of their own in the hills around town.

They stayed in Austin for over a year, until my father's job ran out. My mother traveled to Reno in September 1935 and October 1936, first to give birth to my sister and then to me at Washoe County General Hospital. My mother often told the story, laughingly, of how my father drove her up and down bumpy, dirt roads along the Truckee River, trying to induce labor so I would be born on the weekend, before he had to head back to Austin for work. Despite the jouncing, I stubbornly stayed in the womb until Monday.

Recovery from the Great Depression had begun, but employment, especially in the mining industry, remained uncertain and often short-lived. My parents, sister, and I spent the fall and winter of 1937–38 in a tent house, one of half a dozen that comprised the entire population of the ironically named settlement of Manhattan, Nevada. Once a week, we drove some seventy miles south to Tonopah, the closest town of any size, for supplies.

The spring of 1938 brought a new move, this time north to another failing settlement called Germania, in northeastern

Epilogue

Washington. During our brief stay in Germania, my brother was born in Spokane, the closest town with a hospital. That job lasted only a few months, until, in the late fall of 1938, my father secured a position with the Federal Mining and Smelting Company as assistant superintendent of the Morning Mine, in Mullan, Idaho, the first town west of the Montana-Idaho border as you drove from Missoula to Spokane on old Highway 10.

In those early years of movement and uncertainty, my parents viewed their ups and downs as a great adventure. New people and places excited and stimulated them. My father had grown up in the outdoors, and the West suited his skills and nature. Confident, assertive, and a hard worker, he willingly took the jobs he could find. A well-trained engineer, he applied himself to new challenges with a will. He invested himself in the world of mining and smelting—what he admiringly called "the extractive industries"—and made it his life's work.

My mother, for all her urban upbringing and family attachments, took to her life in the West like the proverbial duck to water. She became an expert at camping, hiking, fishing, and shooting. Later in life, she loved to tell stories of the winter in Manhattan. At bedtime, my parents would stoke the wood stove until it glowed. We would fall contentedly asleep in its warmth, but in the morning, my mother would wake to find everything covered with frost and me still asleep in a wet diaper turned to ice.

Pack rats abounded in the space under the wooden flooring, so my parents banked the canvas walls with canned goods to thwart their entry. All the same, my mother kept the old Remington pump-action .22 at hand to ward off the intruders if need be. I have a black-and-white photo of her standing outside the tent house in the snow, rifle under her arm and a smile on her face. I also have a picture from our time in Idaho of her standing thigh-deep in midstream, fly casting in the St. Regis River. Whether in sagebrush desert or the Rocky Mountains, she had found her home.

Finally, in the northern panhandle of Idaho, some geographical stability arrived for our family. For the next twelve years, we put down roots in Mullan, and then in Wallace, a scant seven miles down the road. We three children went to school, joined youth groups, and played sports. Our parents became active in the communities. They socialized and they joined, and sometimes even led, civic and religious organizations.

World War II brought a final conclusion to the economic depression. The mines producing lead, zinc, and silver proved vital to the war effort and the towns thrived. Mullan, with a population of one thousand, claimed two grocery stores, two drugstores, a clothing store, two barbershops, a beauty parlor, a movie theater, several bars, and even more churches. Two adjacent brick buildings housed the elementary, junior high, and high schools. Wallace, with a population of over three thousand, boasted even more amenities than Mullan, including two hotels, a baseball field, a hospital, a Catholic school, and at least one house of prostitution.

For several years, the family thrived, but over time this stability proved unsustainable. Cracks, eventually unrepairable, began to appear in my parents' previously harmonious union. My father's infidelity and my mother's emasculating resentment soured their relationship and damaged the whole family. In addition, with the end of the war, the mines slowly fell on less prosperous times. The demand for metals slackened.

In the early summer of 1950, my father lost his job yet again, and once more we were on the move. My parents had set a healthy model; we all viewed the upset as one more adventure.

Whatever fears and anxiety my parents may have harbored, they disguised them well. They energetically went about selling the house, putting our belongings in storage, buying a car, and kenneling our dog, after which we set off south, to Salt Lake City, where my father attended a national mining conference in search of new employment. The results of that search landed us in Bauer for one year, a brief stopover on our way to Henderson, Nevada.

My father received a trainee's wage that year in Bauer, and we endured straitened financial circumstances, but not destitution. I had worked in Wallace mowing lawns, shoveling walks, and delivering papers. I paid some of my own expenses, including the mere five dollars it took to buy that magnificent fireworks set. I offered to contribute my savings to our grocery and coal bills, but my mother categorically refused my help.

Better economic times lay ahead in Henderson, at that time a separate town of about twelve thousand. (It has now been completely absorbed by Las Vegas.) My father again earned a regular salary as he directed the construction and operation of a manganese refinery. He became the president of the local Rotary Club, my mother seemed happier, and my sister, brother, and I did well in school and social activities. For the three years we remained in Henderson, even the rift between my mother and father closed somewhat. We enjoyed a period of relative stability and concord.

That amity ended, however, when I finished high school and headed to college a year after my sister had departed. My father had completed his task in Nevada, and he, my mother, and brother relocated to Salt Lake City, a more expensive and less hospitable place for them to live. Neither the marriage nor my father's job survived that final move and all of us went our various ways.

Over the decades, geographical separation became our norm, a striking difference from the way we stuck together as a unit during all the disruptions of the early years. My father stayed in Salt Lake City for the rest of his life. After attending school in Illinois, my sister married and moved to New York, relocating from town to town there for the remainder of her all-too-short life. My mother continued in Henderson for a few years after my brother finished high school, then relocated to San Francisco, then New York, before settling in Phoenix, Arizona, where she spent her final years. My brother went from California to Washington, DC, back to California, to Alaska, and finally to Texas. My path swerved as well, from California for school and the navy, to New York City, to Moscow, Russia, to Rhode Island, New York, Massachusetts, and finally Wyoming. Settling

Epilogue

down takes some time for our family, and we land far apart, but I have now lived in the same house for twenty-one years and hope to stay put.

My two earlier books fill in much of the crucial detail of the family years and of my life as an adult, with its own personal turmoil and balance. Interested readers may turn especially to *The Old Bison: Threads from the Fabric of a Western Life* (Fulton Books, 2022). Stories from my later life in the Mountain West as the parent of two daughters appear in *Three White Pelicans: Stories for Stephanie and Deirdre* (Deep Wild Press, 2021).

Acknowledgments

Two of these stories have previously appeared in print: "My Sister Had an Arvin Radio" and "Not Kissing Carol Druby Goodnight" were published in *The Old Bison* (Fulton Books, 2022).

Joel Fletcher, Rick Kempa, Stephanie Lottridge, and Frankie McCarthy have read some of these stories and commented on them supportively.

I have read several of these pieces to members of the Jackson Hole Artists and Writers group, whose responses have encouraged my work.

Thanks to Janice Harris, who has read several of them gladly and closely. Her suggestions have led me to reconsider passages that might otherwise have remained unclear. Her enthusiastic interest has buoyed me greatly.

Thanks to Anne Muller, longtime friend and fellow artist, who has read all of these tales and offered profoundly sensitive responses and careful observations throughout. Her unfailing support has been instrumental in pulling me forward to complete this book.

As always, thanks to Liz Prax, who formatted the book—a task beyond my ability—and provided acute, detailed editorial suggestions that have refined the text significantly. Her help and aquiline eye have improved this book markedly.

My thanks to Justin Bracken, acquisitions editor at the University of Utah Press, who attentively and skillfully shepherded this book through the approval process. His positive support and energy reassured me at each step of the way.

Finally, my thanks to my copy editor, Dale Topham, and to all the staff at the University of Utah Press. Their attentiveness and expertise have contributed in ways beyond enumerating to the final production of *The Book of Bauer*.

Understanding that no human creation is perfect, I claim any mistakes in this book as my own.

About the Author

Stephen S. Lottridge is a former professor of Slavic languages and literatures and a retired clinical psychologist, with degrees from Stanford and Columbia universities and the Massachusetts School of Professional Psychology. He taught at Brown, Harvard, and other northeastern universities. In 1998, he returned to his native mountain and sagebrush West, settling in Wyoming. A resident of Jackson, he is the father of three children. He is an actor, director, and playwright, as well as the author of essays and poetry. His work has appeared in print journals, anthologies, and online. He received the 2017 Fellowship in Creative Nonfiction from the Wyoming Arts Council. His previous two books are: *Three White Pelicans: Stories for Stephanie and Deirdre* (Deep Wild Press, 2021) and *The Old Bison: Threads from the Fabric of a Western Life* (Fulton Books, 2022).